ULTIMATE
CLASSIC
YACHTS

ULTIMATE CLASSIC YACHTS

20 of the World's Most Beautiful Classic Yachts

Nic Compton

ADLARD COLES NAUTICAL

BLOOMSBURY

LONDON · NEW DELHI · NEW YORK · SYDNEY

Adlard Coles Nautical
An imprint of Bloomsbury Publishing Plc

50 Bedford Square   1385 Broadway
London   New York
WC1B 3DP   NY 10018
UK   USA

www.bloomsbury.com

ADLARD COLES, ADLARD COLES
NAUTICAL and the Buoy logo are
trademarks of Bloomsbury Publishing Plc

First published 2015

British Library Cataloguing-in-Publication
Data
A catalogue record for this book is
available from the British Library.

HB: 978-1-4729-1812-3
ePDF: 978-1-4729-2648-7
ePub: 978-1-4729-2647-0

2 46 81097531

Art Editor Louise Turpin.
Typeset in 10pt Metro.

Printed and bound in China by
C&C Offset Printing Co

Bloomsbury Publishing Plc makes every
effort to ensure that the papers used
in the manufacture of our books are
natural, recyclable products made from
wood grown in well-managed forests.
Our manufacturing processes conform
to the environmental regulations of the
country of origin.

To find out more about our authors
and books visit www.bloomsbury.com.
Here you will find extracts, author
interviews, details of forthcoming
events and the option to sign up for
our newsletters.

CONTENTS

INTRODUCTION

One of the fun things about studying journalism at City University in London was seeing what all your classmates got up to afterwards. Every year, a magazine was sent to the course alumni with updates of people's careers – and the university boasts a high rate of success. In my year alone, one student went on to become head of current affairs at the BBC, another became a news anchor with BBC South, while several joined the *Guardian* and other major newspapers. By contrast, I got a job with *Classic Boat*, a specialist boating magazine based in landlocked Croydon.

But although my career didn't appear as glamorous or well paid as my course mates', there were definite compensations. While most of them were tapping away at computers in the bowels of Broadcasting House or scurrying around meeting daily deadlines, my specialist knowledge meant that I was soon reporting on classic boat events around the world – especially once I left the office and went freelance in 2000. Before long, I was being paid (or at least getting expenses) to attend events such as the Australian Wooden Boat Festival in Tasmania, the Raja Muda Selangor Regatta in Malaysia, the Régates Impériales in Ajaccio and other regattas in places as varied as New Zealand, Antigua, Hong Kong, Maine, Scotland, the South of France and Scandinavia.

Which is where the material for this book comes from. Over the past 20 years, I have sailed on dozens of classic yachts in at least 20 countries. I've sailed on no-expense-spared restorations such as the exquisite Fife 15-Metre *The Lady Anne* (see page 54), massively ambitious replicas such as the 136-foot (41.5-metre) Herreshoff schooner *Eleonora* (see page 142), and more humble home-built craft such as the delightful 24-foot (7.3-metre) *Madoc* (see page 128). What has struck me each time is that these boats all have a story to tell. Even if they haven't made epic journeys (which many of them have) or won major races (ditto), there are usually stories in their designs or their making – or simply in their ability to survive (viz *Rawene* (see page 48) and *Solway Maid* (see page 100), mothballed for 20 and 14 years, respectively). For these are not just boats; they are personalities.

There's no doubt the classic yacht movement has come a long way since my first article was published in *Classic Boat* in 1991. I recently sailed on a 37-foot yacht built in 1962 by a relatively unknown designer, which someone had just spent £280,000 restoring – a sum that would have been unthinkable 20 years ago for a boat that size, even for one of the big 'names' such as Fife and Herreshoff. The owner knows he'll get his money back, and more, when he sells, because of the prestige value of owning a genuine classic yacht.

But there's danger in spending too much on an old wooden boat – replacing and rebuilding rather than mending and restoring. It's all very well creating a beautiful yacht, but if that means losing the original fabric of the vessel for the sake of looking good on the quay at St Tropez, then we really are throwing the baby out with the bathwater. Which is why you'll see a lot of emphasis on originality in these pages, especially in restorations such as *Lulworth* (see page 62). I'd rather see a boat that carries the scars of its past with pride than a boat rebuilt 'in the spirit' of the past but which is essentially new.

Nic Compton

PARTRIDGE (1885)

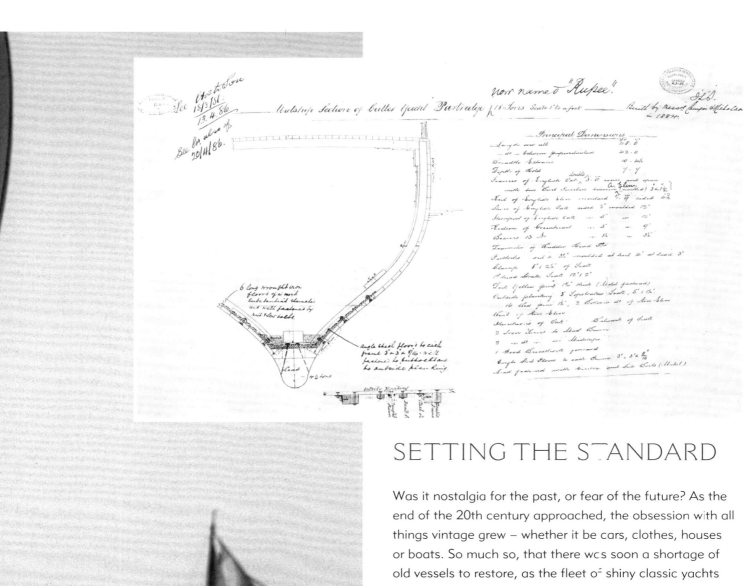

SETTING THE STANDARD

Was it nostalgia for the past, or fear of the future? As the end of the 20th century approached, the obsession with all things vintage grew – whether it be cars, clothes, houses or boats. So much so, that there was soon a shortage of old vessels to restore, as the fleet of shiny classic yachts steadily grew. Not all were adored in equal measure, however, and some inevitably stood out from the crowd. In 1993, it was the William Fife-designed cutter *Tuiga* that wowed the crowds when she appeared at the Nioulargue Regatta in St Tropez, fresh from a comprehensive rebuild on the Hamble. A year later, it was the turn of the 1896 Camper & Nicholsons cutter *Avel* to dazzle, with her unusual clipper bow and acres of varnish.

As the millennium came to a close, another British yacht became the focus of attention: a 49-foot (14.9-metre) gaff cutter called *Partridge*, newly arrived on the circuit after an astonishing 18-year restoration. Anyone who attended the Mediterranean classic yacht regattas in 1999 could not

ABOVE: Details of the floor construction drawn for Lloyd's in 1885.

LEFT: Partridge *enjoys a breeze off Cannes, after her 75-year hibernation.*

fail to notice the new arrival, with her distinctive plumb (ie vertical) bow, her long counter stern and her slightly austere manner. She looked like a vessel that had sailed across time from another era, which is exactly what she was.

Not only that, but she was surprisingly fast. From the moment *Partridge* beat *Avel* in the Conde de Barcelona Regatta in Mallorca, the races became a battle between these two iconic yachts, with the new kid on the block invariably finishing first. By the end of the season, *Partridge* had accumulated an embarrassing number of trophies, including overall first at Monaco and first in her class at Mallorca and St Tropez. But what made the yacht truly outstanding was not her undoubted beauty nor her unexpected speed, but the story behind her painstaking restoration.

Alex Laird was 19 and working as an apprentice at the Fairey Marine boatyard in East Cowes when he got a letter from his uncle Peter Saxby saying, 'I wonder whether you would be interested in the following proposition: we buy an old boat, you do it up.' It was an irresistible offer for a young man fascinated by wooden boats and yacht construction, and he immediately set out to find a suitable candidate. It would have been easy enough to find any old gaff cutter and do it up, but Alex had his eyes set on something more substantial. 'I was looking for a hull with special lines, with a special shape that would need considerable work to restore, and with lots of potential,' he said.

A few weeks later he headed for the east coast of England where, he had been told, there were still a number of old hulls lying in the sand and mud, left prey to the elements. And indeed a large chunk of British maritime culture lay in those muddy creeks, often converted into houseboats. Priceless historic yachts such as *Avel*, *Mariquita* and *Hispania* were all dug out of the mud there and given extravagant restorations, before joining the classic yacht circuit.

After looking at about 15 abandoned boats in various stages of dereliction, Alex spotted a black hull in a small tributary of the Blackwater River in Essex, propped up by a few wooden posts. He knew at once by the shape of the boat and by the way the frames and deck beams had been fitted, that it was something out of the ordinary. The current owner warned him the restoration would take at least three years – but then, he didn't know he was dealing with a perfectionist. Peter and Alex paid £400 for the hull, and another £1,000 to have it transported to the backyard of Alex's parents' house in Shalfleet, on the Isle of Wight. He built a roof above it, and went back to his job at Fairey Marine.

It was several years before Alex could get started on the project in earnest but in the meantime he worked at weekends and holidays on the hull, helped by friends and family. The technical college at Newport on the Isle of Wight happened to be launching an intensive one-year boatbuilding course, and the bosses at Fairey Marine agreed to sponsor him on that, followed by a three-year yacht design course at Southampton.

Meanwhile, he started researching the history of the ghost of a boat he had bought. The only clues he had were that, according to the previous owner, she had once been called *Tanagra* and an inscription had been found on an old deck beam, saying: 'Harry, 1885'.

SPECIFICATIONS

LOD: 49ft 2in (14.9m)
LWL: 41ft 7in (12.7m)
Beam: 10ft 5in (3.2m)
Draft: 8ft 5in (2.6m)
Displacement: 28 tons
Sail area: 2,690sq ft (250m²)

RIGHT: As Alex found her, on the Blackwater River in Essex.

THIS PICTURE: Sailing off the Isle of Wight soon after being restored.

As he searched through Lloyd's Register of Shipping, Alex found a yacht called *Tanagra* with more or less the same dimensions as his hull, registered in 1923. The list of earlier names took him back to *Pollie*, *Rupee* and, at last, *Partridge* of 1885 – the same year in which a certain Harry, no doubt one of the workers at the yard, carved his name on a deck beam. To his (and Peter Saxby's) relief, the registration proved the boat was indeed something out of the ordinary. *Partridge* was designed by J Beavor-Webb, who the same year drew the lines of the America's Cup challenger *Galatea*, and was built by the famous Camper & Nicholsons yard in Gosport. Peter and Alex had stumbled on their own chapter of maritime history.

As Alex later wrote: 'Instinct had led us to a vesse put together by people who knew what they were doing and had an eye for the perfect line.'

Further research revealed fragments of the yacht's past. Between 1885 and 1924, she had 14 owners, a turnover rate which was quite normal at that time, when owners often had a boat for just one season before trying out another. Thus it was that her original name, *Partridge*, was changed to *Rupee* after just one year. On 17 July 1886, she competed in a regatta at the Royal Torbay Yacht Club, but no special triumphs are recorded. Her last trace was in the 1923 Lloyd's Register, which stated she had been sold to a Belgian who had converted her into a houseboat – not an unusual end for a wooden yacht after a 38-year career.

When Alex found the derelict hull in August 1980, there was nothing left of the interior, rig, deck or lead keel. But the teak and pitch pine hull planking was practically intact, and most of the framework had survived and had helped retain her shape over the years. Alex was still studying naval architecture when he started measuring the hull. He drafted the deck layout and sail plan and made more than 25 drawings of the yacht's deck gear and other details. 'It was very useful to have this period of reflection to think about what lay ahead,' he said. 'It meant that, when I did start the work, I was able to do everything in the right order, with a clear view of what needed to be done.'

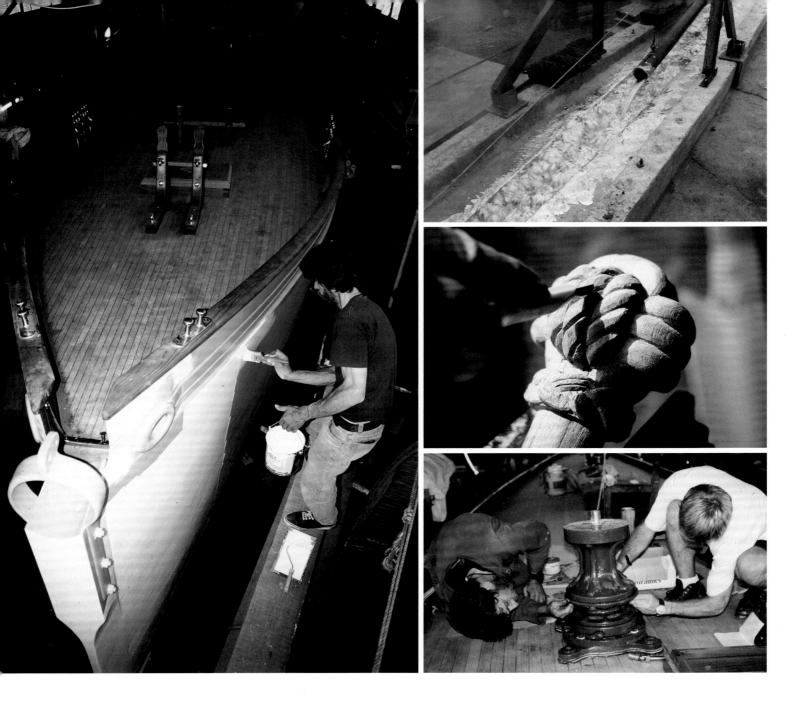

With no original drawings or photos available, designing the myriad details of the deck and rig was a matter of detailed research – and an element of guesswork. Alex was also able to refer to and cross-reference with *Avel* and *Marigold*, two Nicholson cutters being restored at about the same time. Coincidentally, one of *Partridge*'s owners during the 19th century had also owned *Marigold*. In turn, Alex played a significant role in *Marigold*'s life by persuading her restorer, Greg Powlesland, to enter his yacht into a special auction at Sotheby's, where she found new owners who would fund her entire restoration.

Alex not only made detailed drawings of *Partridge*'s anatomy, he also made a 1: 15 scale model. The idea was to have a project to keep him going through any low points in the restoration, but it also allowed him to optimise details of the deck and rigging. His plan was to lay the deck planks full length, from bow to stern, tapering them to match the deck's elliptical shape. It was a tricky task which he thought he'd best try on a model first.

Alex, aided by his ever-growing team of helpers, did a large part of the physical work himself too, from casting the nine-ton keel (4.75 tons heavier

TOP LEFT: The finished hull gets a lick of paint.

TOP RIGHT: Pouring molten lead into the ballast keel mould.

CENTRE: Carving the tiller end.

BOTTOM RIGHT : A vintage capstan was mounted on the foredeck.

TOP: Looking forward, prior to restoration.

BOTTOM: Same view after restoration, complete with minimalist interior.

than the original, to replace the internal ballast he had removed so as to make way for fuel tanks in the bilges) to making the spars and shaping the new oak frames. All the deck gear and hull fittings were cast in nickel-aluminium-bronze, to Alex's moulds, while the mast and rigging gear were all fabricated in steel and galvanised.

A 40hp Lister Petter engine was fitted, turning two propellers via a hydraulic drive. Alex decided this was a better option than the usual centrally mounted engine and propeller, as the engine could be located anywhere in the boat. And it's certainly a sympathetic option for a classic old dame not intended to carry such a newfangled gadget as a diesel engine.

There were, inevitably, moments when Alex felt overwhelmed by the sheer scale of the project, and he thought he would have to quit. 'After three months' work, I had rebuilt half of the frames. I looked forward and saw all the new frames, then I looked aft and saw all the rotten ones, and I realised I would need another three months just to finish this part of the restoration. It was devastating. But I was in the happy position of not being under pressure commercially-speaking. So I could leave the work for a while, and go back to it with renewed enthusiasm a few weeks later.'

Finally, on 4 June 1998, three-quarters of a century after being de-rigged and turned into a houseboat, *Partridge* heeled to the breeze once again. It must have been an emotional moment when she sailed past Gosport that day, the very place where a shipwright called Harry had carved his name on her deck beam more than a century before.

By then, Alex had hammered some 3,000 copper nails into the hull, eight oak trees had been used for the frames alone, 2,500 feet (780 metres) of teak had been turned into deck planking, five red pine trees had been turned into mast and spars, and 72 blocks had been made to control her sails. Alex himself was by then 38 and an absolute authority on wooden boat restoration. With a project of that magnitude on his CV, he would never have trouble finding work.

'Looking back, I can safely say ignorance is bliss,' Alex wrote. 'Had we known what lay ahead, we undoubtedly would have shied away from it all. Everything we worked on was done to the highest standards we could achieve, so I have never regretted not taking any of those short cuts that often were horribly tempting…'

The total cost of the restoration, including her first season's racing, was about half a million pounds. But that was with a basic 'racing' fit-out, with no watertight bulkheads and just canvas cots to sleep on. The full accommodation would follow later, perhaps.

Shortly before *Partridge* was craned onto the deck of a container ship bound for the south of France, I was invited to sail on her for a day. The young crew was well trained in managing the almost 2,100 square feet (195 square metres) of sail area. As we headed down the Solent on a downwind course, Alex invited me to take the helm. A gust of wind made deep ripples in the black water, and *Partridge* accelerated without seeming to heel at all. The helm was steady and easy. Despite her length of almost 50 feet (15 metres) and a draft of 8 feet 5 inches (2.60 metres), the yacht felt light. But how fast would she really be? It was hard to tell with no competition around. The yacht had excellent pedigree, but would she be that extra half knot faster, which you can barely notice while cruising but which would be the deciding factor in any regatta? As it turned out, I needn't have worried. Soon after, *Partridge* proved that Alex had not only stayed faithful to the yacht's past but in the process had also managed to optimise her sailing performance. *Partridge*'s second life was off to a flying start.

'The most exciting moment for me was when we rounded the first mark in Palma, with a lead on *Avel* and her experienced captain and crew. I knew then she was fast,' Alex said later. 'The most emotional moment was when Prince Albert of Monaco handed Peter Saxby the trophies for the *concours d'élégance* and the Best Restoration at the Monaco Classic Week in 1999. It was amazing to think all the people who had watched us sailing from land had judged *Partridge* the most beautiful and the most authentically restored yacht in the fleet.

'When Peter bought the boat, my younger sister was ten years old. When she finally came sailing on board, she was almost 30. When you think about that … it's just scary.'

RIGHT: Free as a bird, after her 18-year restoration.

What happened next…

Partridge proved almost unbeatable in her first season on the Mediterranean, winning three of the four regattas she attended. She went on to win the Vele d'Epoca regatta at Imperia the following year and repeated her success in 2014, winning Les Voiles de St Tropez. Alex worked as project manager on two more major restorations before co-founding the Classic Works boatyard in La Ciotat, France, in 2003. The yard now employs 15 shipwrights and has a clientele of more than 500 yachts. Peter Saxby died in 2013, and *Partridge* was bought by his friend Jean-Raymond Boulle, who helped finance the latter part of her restoration. Alex still manages, oversees and occasionally sails *Partridge* for her new owner.

MARIAN (1889)

THE TALE OF THE LAZY PILOT

The legend of the Bristol Channel pilots and their vessels, the hardy pilot cutters, is entrenched in British nautical folklore. The Bristol Channel, we are constantly reminded, is one of the most dangerous shipping lanes in the world, littered with dangerous sand bars and rocks and cursed with extreme tides and weather to match. The vessels which evolved to cope with these conditions and deliver the pilots safely to approaching ships at all times of the year and in any weather have rightly earned a reputation for speed and seaworthiness. Equally, the men who sailed these boats, the legendary Westernmen, and the pilots they worked with have acquired almost iconic status as brave and competent seamen.

ABOVE: As Colaba, *after being converted to a yacht.*

RIGHT: Sailing on the Carrick Roads, off Falmouth, after restoration.

John H Morse, it seems, was a little bit different. Born in Cardiff in 1861, he came from a family of Bristol Channel seafarers, and both his father and his grandfather were Cardiff pilots. Having served his apprenticeship and worked as a first class port pilot, on July 1896 he qualified as a Channel pilot – the ultimate qualification, allowing him to work the entire Bristol Channel. From his pilot's licence, we learn that he lived at 26 High Street in Penarth (next to Cardiff), that he served his apprenticeship in Toabaiaiff Tieoi (not found on any modern maps), and that he served in the overseas trade for two years. The register of pilots also contains a brief description of the man: 'Height 5ft 4in, brown hair, brown beard, blue eyes, fresh complexion.'

The 1891 census reveals that John Henry Morse was married to Margaret and that they had, at that time, five children: Marian, Ethel, Mary, Winifred and John. Tantalisingly, the register of pilots states that he owned his own boat, but doesn't give the name of the vessel, while other vital pilotage records were lost when they were used as infill for a new dock. From earlier censuses, however, we learn that his mother and his grandmother were called Marian and Mary Ann respectively, while other records show that his grandfather was 'Owner and Master' of a vessel by the name of *Mary Ann*. Circumstantial evidence, therefore, points to John Henry Morse being the owner of the pilot cutter *Marian*, built by Hambly & Sons in Cardiff in 1889.

Far from being the noble master of the Western Approaches, however, JH Morse seems to have been something of a reluctant, and even recalcitrant, pilot. The minute books of the Cardiff Pilotage Board are full of claims for 'disputed Pilotage' by Morse against various rival pilots — particularly one RS Reid and one JW Reid, with whom he seems to have had ongoing feuds. In most instances, the Board finds against Morse. An entry for 8 January 1895, for instance, finds Morse complaining that James Reid boarded the *SS Nethergate* even though he himself 'was first in turn to the westward when the vessel bound up'. Reid responds by accusing Morse of being slow off the mark and still being at anchor when he himself set off. The Board apparently agrees, awards the pilotage to Reid and raps Morse for 'want of alertness'.

And it seems that JH Morse was, perhaps in common with many of his ilk, not the mildest mannered sailor on the Bristol Channel. At least twice in the minutes he is censured for 'abusive language' and ordered to apologise to the ship's captain.

But perhaps the worst indictment of Morse's tenure as pilot comes on 7 April 1901. By then a veteran pilot with over 20 years' experience, he decided to take on an apprentice. First, however, he had to get approval of the Board. After giving his request due consideration, the board concluded that 'Morse had, for some years, confined himself to working vessels coming from the eastwards and seldom if ever went to the westwards deck for ships'. In other words, rather than venturing out into the wilds of the Western Approaches, Morse was hanging out at the eastward end of the Channel waiting for easier pickings from Bristol and Avonmouth, in the hope of being back in time for tea. This, they said, was not conducive to best practice in the Pilotage Services and 'would

SPECIFICATIONS

LOD: 50ft (15.2m)
LWL: 44ft (13.4m)
Beam: 12ft 10in (3.9m)
Draft: 7ft 9in (2.4m)
Displacement: 27.6 tons
Sail area: 1,613sq ft (150m²)

seriously prejudice the apprentice's chance when he came to apply
for a licence'.

Morse's application was refused and only a written appeal from him
assuring the Board that he would sail more 'to the westward' eventually
persuaded them to approve the request.

After a final spat of disputed pilotage between one JL Harvey and
JH Morse, the minutes note on 6 July 1915: 'The Clerk reported the death
of John Henry Morse, First Class Pilot.' He was just 54. Some months later,
Mrs JH Morse is reported as applying 'for the usual annuity' out of the
pilotage funds – presumably a reference to a widow's pension – and is duly
awarded £18.17 per year (equivalent to around £1,800/2,100 euros now).

But, while Morse may not have been the most courageous or the most
polite pilot in the Bristol Channel, he must have done something right,
for his charge, the cutter *Marian*, survived his custody and survived well
enough that, when sail eventually did give way to steam and the vessel's
working life was finally over, she was not automatically scrapped. Many
other pilot cutters were not so lucky. All those years thrashing it out in the
Western Approaches took their toll on the best-built craft and many ended
up abandoned to the mud or chopped up into firewood.

Marian was nearly a quarter of a century old when Morse died. What
happened next is unclear, but at some point in the late 1910s or early
1920s she was converted into a yacht – including, in a symbolic break with
her working-boat past, being painted white. It was a time when yachtsmen
were starting to make serious ocean voyages, several of which were written
up in landmark books which would subsequently sow the seeds for a whole
generation of 'cruising' nomads. One such was the Norwegian Erling
Tambs, whose 1933 book *The Cruise of the Teddy* describes a trip to the
Pacific aboard his converted Colin Archer pilot boat *Teddy*. Inspired by the
book, aircraft designer Johnny Aherne-Heron bought *Marian* – by then
renamed *Colaba* – intending to sail the ocean blue. World War II exploded
those dreams, however, and instead of frolicking amid the atolls, *Marian*
found herself slumped against the King's Quay in Brixham, with the tide
washing in and out of her.

She was spotted there in 1961 by William Taylor, an enthusiastic young
television producer-to-be with minimal knowledge of sailing but a great
love of the sea, who bought her with £500 loaned to him by his landlady's
sister. He pumped the boat out and got her sailing again for a couple of
years, even managing to get her a small part in a Michael Winner movie
being filmed in Brixham, before family life and career forced him to sell her
on. Like many others of her ilk, she was eventually de-rigged and turned
into a houseboat back on the Hamble, suffering the usual indignities in the
process. One owner, simply known as 'Fibreglass Bill', smothered her in the
sticky stuff – an act which would nowadays be met with derision but which
nevertheless seems to have helped preserve her for a few more years.

*LEFT: Pilot cutters had to be seaworthy and fast to
sail the Bristol Channel in all weathers and reach
the ships before their rivals.*

TOP: *Being craned out of the water at Gweek, prior to restoration.*

BOTTOM: *The hull is ready – time to get the deck on!*

Marian's fortunes, in common with those of many traditional boats, began to look up in the 1980s. At about the same time as her much grander neighbour, the J-Class yacht *Endeavour*, was dragged out of her mud berth and taken to Holland for a multimillion-dollar restoration, *Marian* also slipped her mooring for the first time in decades. Her eight-year restoration at the hands of Peter Stuysted was an altogether less elaborate affair, however, than that of the 'Darling Jade'. The main priority was to get the boat out of the mud and sailing again, based on the well-founded theory that 'a boat sailed is a boat saved'. By now, being an authentic working boat was regarded as something to be proud of, and her 'yachty' white livery was abandoned in favour of a traditional black hull, with red trim.

By the time Dominic Ziegler came across her, she had changed hands once again and was lying under cover up the River Helford in Cornwall, awaiting a saviour. After a childhood knocking about on the Hamble River – mostly racing Mirrors, Lasers and, later, IOR boats – Dom had been instilled with romantic memories of the former great dames of the sea languishing in various corners of the river. Working as foreign correspondent for the *Economist* living in China, he began to long for something quintessentially English to come home to. And what more quintessentially English than a British Channel pilot cutter?

A survey revealed that, while the boat would need a complete rebuild at some point in the next few years, she would be OK for a bit of coastal sailing until then. Just how delicate the boat was became apparent one day as Dom was sailing around Land's End. 'You could tell she was changing shape because on one tack the latch for the loo door was too high to lock it, and on the other tack it was too low!' The solution, Dom concluded, was to make sure there was always at least one shipwright on board whenever he went sailing.

After three years' coastal sailing in south-west England and Brittany, Dom decided the time had come to bite the bullet. Simply handing the boat over to a boatyard to do the work wasn't an option, however – Dom's salary simply didn't stretch to that. Instead, he rented a space at Gweek Quay Boatyard and employed a team of Cornish boatbuilders, led by David Walkey, to do the job. And, long before that, he started collecting the necessary materials. Oak logs for the frames were stacked up and left to season, and thousands of specialist fastenings and fittings were sourced. 'It was lovely to contemplate this going on from the far side of the world,' says Dom. 'It was all part of the anticipation.'

Although the boat would end up being completely rebuilt, it was important to Dom that she looked as much as possible like she did when she was a working boat, rather than when she was a yacht. Fortunately, photos dating from immediately after her conversion showed the position of deck fittings and the flush-deck arrangement before the cabin trunks were added. And the vessel had miraculously retained many of her original deck fittings, which simply had to be refurbished and put back. Below decks, there was nothing left of the original accommodation, so the new interior was based on the classic pilot cutter arrangement of crew quarters and galley up forward, with the navigation area aft and pilot berths (yes, genuine 'pilot' berths!) in the saloon and table to port.

Ten thousand man hours and several trees later, *Marian* was relaunched in autumn 2002 – this time in an elegant two-tone blue which, in a typical 21st-century compromise, shouts out neither 'working boat' nor 'yacht'. Dom, meanwhile, was appointed to a new post in Japan and his plans to go cruising had to go on the back burner. Instead, under the name of the Real Boat Company, *Marian* was chartered from her base in Mylor on the River Fal, with former underwater diver-turned-yacht-skipper Jim Goddard at the helm.

And they received a visit from a past owner: William Taylor, the TV producer who saved her from the King's Quay in Brixham in 1961. He stumbled on the boat while she was being restored in Gweek, and subsequently visited her in Mylor on his own boat, a fibreglass cruising yacht called *Spirit of Colaba*. For his 70th birthday, his family hooked up with Dom to organise a surprise outing on *Marian*, along with various

TOP LEFT: The hull was gutted before work could commence.

BOTTOM LEFT: Almost none of the hull timber was salvageable.

TOP RIGHT: New frames were shaped out of oak…

BOTTOM RIGHT: … and new planks cut out of Scottish larch.

members of William's family and an old friend from those Brixham days.

Meanwhile, Dom was still rehearsing the arguments around *Marian*'s restoration. 'There are those who object to the fact that the boat has been so completely rebuilt,' he said, with a pained expression. 'But it does mean that she can be sailed just as hard as everyone else, and it means we can go cruising without having to worry about seams opening up the whole time. I am sure it was the right thing to do…'

You get the feeling that, even while he is interviewing Japanese leaders about whether China will go to war over the disputed Senkaku Islands, he will still be thinking about how to adjust the sheeting angle of *Marian*'s jib or whether carrying an outboard engine for the dinghy is really in keeping with the spirit of the boat. For while the boat's horizons have widened since John Morse's days, the issues remain largely unchanged. And no doubt the old pilot is happily swearing in his grave about that.

Historical research courtesy of Hannah Cunliffe www.researchthepast.com

What happened next…

When skipper Jim gave up the sea to become a horse whisperer, *Marian* was entrusted to the care of local sailor John Gyll-Murray and started a new life cruising the West Country, Brittany and Ireland with the Friends of Marian. She became a regular competitor at the Pilot Cutter Race in St Mawes, where she achieved her best result in 2011, coming 4th overall out of 11 boats.

RIGHT:
The interior was completely scrapped and rebuilt.

FAR RIGHT TOP: Owner Dominic Ziegler at the helm, with some of the Friends of Marian on board.

BOTTOM: With four sails to set on a typical pilot cutter, there are plenty of bits of string to play with…

According to legend, the first Bristol Channel pilot was George James Ray who, in May 1497, piloted John Cabot's *Matthew* out of Bristol on her voyage to the Americas. Bristol was then an extremely important port, and the pilots based at the mouth of the River Avon, which provided the only access for ships, had a stranglehold over incoming traffic. The town of Pill, in particular, has been synonymous with pilotage for 450 years and is still home to pilots who can trace their ancestors back to the earliest days of the profession. The Bristol pilots held a monopoly over the entire Bristol Channel until 1861, when the ports of Cardiff, Newport and Gloucester were finally allowed to appoint their own pilots.

The pilot cutter Cariad *worked under sail until 1922.*

Even before the Bristol monopoly was broken, however, pilots operated independently of each other and competition to get work was intense. Pilots had to be on hand to meet incoming ships at any time of day and in any kind of weather – in fact, the worse the weather, the more their services were required. The boats they sailed therefore had to be fast enough to beat their rivals, sturdy enough to withstand years of pounding in the Atlantic swell and handy enough to be manoeuvred by one man. The result was a cutter-rigged vessel, usually 50–60 feet long, with a plumb stem and long counter, as handsome as it was seaworthy.

Transferring the pilot from one boat to the other was the most dangerous part of the operation. Sometimes this was done by simply coming alongside, although in rough weather this was particularly hazardous and there are records of pilots falling and being crushed to death. More commonly, the pilot cutter would sail in the lee of the ship and the apprentice would row the pilot over in a rowboat, leaving the skipper to man the cutter alone. The danger then was that the ship might drift down onto the cutter, stealing its wind and crushing it. On one occasion, a steamship cut straight through a pilot cutter, leaving its crew hanging on to the steamer's anchors for dear life!

BONA FIDE (1899)

TIME TRAVELLER

The Italian summer was already well under way in the Italian seaside town of Porto Santo Stefano when a familiar ritual began to take place. It wasn't the blossoming of the bougainvillea or the children swimming from the end of the pier – though that was happening too – but the launch of the latest classic yacht at the Cantiere Navale dell'Argentario. Since the mid 1990s, the yard had developed an enviable reputation for bringing back to life a string of fine vintage yachts, mostly of American extraction, including such stars as *Dorade*, *Stormy Weather* (see page 76), *Nyala*, *Sonny* and *Cholita*. One by one they came to the yard in various stages of dilapidation and dismemberment and, after a few months under the mindful hands of the *cantiere*'s master craftsmen, reappeared looking beautiful again.

But something strange was happening this time. Whereas in previous years the assembled launch party had been treated to the easy, flowing lines of an Olin Stephens masterpiece, or similar, the yacht on the slipway waiting to be launched looked altogether more modern. Compared with *Stormy Weather*'s slim, wineglass hulls, she was beamy, with an almost flat, canoe underbody and a plain, functional keel. Stranger still, at the bottom of her keel was a gently aerofoiled bulb. It was more akin to the shape of a ULDB (ultra light displacement boat) so beloved of the 1970s onwards, or even of those Open 60s which took the world by storm in the 1990s. Frankly, it was not a pretty sight. What was going on? Had the yard bosses lost the plot?

In truth, the yacht being launched on that occasion was older than all the other boats restored at the *cantiere* by at least 30 years. *Bona Fide*, as she was called, was built on the Isle of Wight in 1899 during a period of unprecedented experimentation and development in yacht design. The Length and Sail Area Rule had been adopted by the Yacht Racing Association in 1887, and the sheer simplicity of the rule allowed designers an enormous degree of freedom to try out new ideas. An early pioneer of the type was Charles Sibbick of Cowes, truly a man before his time. Looking at the keel of one of his 30-foot Linear Raters, with its bulb keel set on a narrow steel plate, you can't help thinking you're looking at a craft from nearly a century later.

Characteristically, when J Howard Taylor asked Sibbick to design a yacht to the Godinet rule then prevalent on the Mediterranean circuit, the designer pushed the envelope

INSET: Bona Fide *winning the first ever Olympic sailing event, in 1900.*

THIS PICTURE: And 100 years later, fully restored, sailing off Cannes.

to the limit. His design was 29ft 2in (8.9m) long on the waterline, with 15ft 5in (4.7m) of overhangs, on a beam of 8ft 5in (2.57m). She had 5,180lb (2,350kg) of her 25,130lb (11,400kg) displacement in her bulb keel and set a vast 1,550sq ft (144m²) of sail. In short, a skimming dish of a yacht. Built in little more than two months, *Bona Fide* was launched in November 1899 – her name no doubt a tongue-in-cheek reference to the fact that although she did qualify as a 'bona fide' 5-tonner, she defied many other 'bona fide' design conventions of the day.

The yacht was immediately taken to Nice and early the following year took part in a series of regattas on the Côte d'Azur between Toulon and Monaco. But the biggest test of her career came six months after she was launched, in May 1900. The newly revived Olympic Games were held in Paris in 1900 and, for the first time, sailing was included. Most of the boating events were held on the Seine, although as the river in Paris itself was too narrow the course was located downriver at Meulan. *Bona Fide*

SPECIFICATIONS

LOA: 44ft 7in (13.60m)
LWL: 29ft 2in (8.9m)
Beam: 8ft 5in (2.57m)
Draft: 1.86m
Displacement: 11.2 tons
Sail area: 1,550sq ft (144m²)

was entered in the 3–10 ton class, along with eight other competitors. The flat waters of the Seine were ideal for Sibbick's trail skimming dish which triumphed despite the tricky fluvial conditions. *Bona Fide* had won Gold in the first ever Olympic sailing race, and duly earned herself a place in the history of the sport.

Despite such auspicious beginnings, Taylor, a man of many yachts, sold *Bona Fide* the following year to Giovanni Brambilla from Milan. Brambilla based the boat on Lake Como in northern Italy and raced her there and on the Côte d'Azur, notching up several notable wins. Even in 1908, by which time most of Europe had switched to the more seaworthy International Rule boats, she was still winning events on her home turf, including the Bellano-Colico-Lecco-Bellano passage race which earned her owner 100 lire in prize money.

By 1915, however, the yacht had disappeared from the records, reappearing only briefly in 1937 in a list of competitors for a race on Lake Maggiore. By then her owner was listed as Count Giovanni Lanza di Mazzarino. The count kept her on Lake Como for a number of years, before selling her in 1962 to two brothers, Jacopo and Cesare Pellegrini. Like so many others of that era, the Pellegrini brothers had little appreciation of the yacht's pedigree and immediately set about altering her to bring her up to date. The old gaff rig was dumped in favour of a Bermudan rig using the mast off an old 8-Metre yacht; the keel was modified and the bulb reduced to 88lb (400kg), presumably to improve her light-weather performance. The brothers did recognise a timeless piece of engineering when they saw it, however, and, when they sold the boat three years later, they kept her original bronze tiller.

In retrospect, it's easy to dismiss their revamp as an act of sacrilege, but in the context of the times it was no more or less than what everyone else was doing. Ultimately, it may have made the difference between keeping the vessel in use, and therefore maintained to basic sailing order, rather than being abandoned to the lichen. And the Pellegrinis contributed to their charge's eventual salvation in another important way: by taking photos of the yacht both before and after her 'modernisation'. Decades later, these images would provide essential clues for her restorers to base their work on.

Bona Fide was apparently still going strong in the mid 1970s, when her new owner had a teak deck fitted on her at a yard on Lake Como. And it was around this time that a wheelhouse was added to her minimal superstructure. It wasn't until the early 1990s, with the classic yacht revival in full swing on the Mediterranean, that the historic significance of the yacht was recognised. In 1993 she was taken to the Cantiere Dalò on Lake Como and *smontato* (ie dismantled) in readiness for a major restoration. And that was it. No more work was done on her for almost ten years.

In the autumn of 1999, Giuseppe Giordano was looking for a new boat. A relative newcomer to sailing, he had just taken part for the first time in the Régates Royales in Cannes aboard his newly restored Laurent Giles cutter *Cerida*. As he steered his new charge through the armada of exquisite yachts, he was particularly captivated by the towering gaff rigs set by some of the other vessels there. Although *Cerida* was a finely crafted yacht of impeccable pedigree, she nevertheless carried her original

BOTTOM LEFT: Despite her age, Bona Fide *is competitive once again.*

BELOW: Many of the original fittings were found, whilst others were faithfully recreated.

Bermudan rig – representing, as it did, the height of fashion when she was launched in 1937. Sixty years on and with the end of the millennium approaching, the fashion was for everything retro, which included good old-fashioned classic boats with good old-fashioned gaff sails. And Giuseppe wanted to join the fun.

Giuseppe discussed his thoughts with Federico Nardi of the Cantiere Navale dell'Argentario, which had worked on the finishing stages of *Cerida's* restoration. Federico and his colleague Doug Peterson (a former America's Cup designer-turned-classic-boat-geek) had caught wind of an unusual boat lying derelict in a warehouse in Milan. Despite the vessel's derelict appearance, the three men agreed she would indeed make a suitable subject for a complete restoration – although, luckily, none of them was in any hurry to get started. One of the side effects of the *smantellamento* was that, with no interior structure to hold her in position, the yacht had lost her lines. The solution was to place her in a framework of trestles and supports and to gradually ease her back into shape using her own weight. It was meticulous and time-consuming work, yielding a change of only about 10mm per week. Not unlike waiting for a good wine to mature.

Although the yard had been unable to track down the original line drawings, Federico was never in any doubt what they were aiming for. 'Once we got to the right shape, all the lines came together,' he said. 'There was only one exact position when that could possibly happen. It took two years to achieve that.' You can almost imagine a choir of angels singing a hallelujah as the hull finally found its original shape – its *only* true shape – and *Bona Fide* was born again.

Meanwhile, Federico and Doug were busy researching the yacht's history, following a trail that would lead them from her birthplace on the Isle of Wight to the Royal Thames Yacht Club, which her original owner was a member of, back to Italy, France and finally Switzerland, where they uncovered valuable information about the yacht's participation in the 1900 Olympics at the organisation's headquarters. The result was a detailed archive tracing the yacht's history as well as a handful of priceless photographs – including the Pellegrinis' before and after snaps – revealing important details of the original rig and fittings.

Once the hull had found its true shape again, the task of rebuilding could begin. First off was the distinctive steel keel, which was regalvanised and fitted with a new bulb cast to the original design using 5,180lb (2,350kg) of lead. Much of the centreline was replaced using Khaya mahogany and the planking renewed with Oregon pine. The underwater hull was resheathed in copper, using many of the original panels. By the time the yard had finished, only a few planks, some floors and the deckbeams were left of the original craft.

Although most of the original fittings were stripped off the boat during the Pellegrini brothers' revamp, their photos of the boat prior to that provided the most useful guidance on the layout of the deck and the position of the deck fittings. Miraculously, several of the original fittings were discovered at the Cantiere Dalò, the *smantellamento* yard itself, including the fairleads, rudder, turnbuckles and dolphin striker. Most

TOP: Most of the old planking had to be replaced.

CENTRE: The controversial fin keel – regalvanised and awaiting a new bulb.

TOP: *There's barely sitting headroom inside* Bona Fide's *shallow, canoe-shaped hull.*

BOTTOM: *The hull was stretched on trestles for several months to bring it back to shape.*

of these were recast to their original patterns, while other fittings were replaced with contemporary hardware (much of it sourced on the internet) or custom-made in the original style. The old Sibbick tiller has yet to be found.

Finding the exact dimensions of the rig also required some investigative nous. The archive photos helped establish the basic proportions, but for the exact dimensions Federico went back to the Godinet rule of 1892. Using the boat's waterline length and her designed sail area, which they knew from their research, they were able to work their way backwards through the formula to arrive at the rig's precise measurements. Then it was back to the old photos for the minutia of mast fittings, block ratios and sail cut.

The usual crowds attended the launch of the Cantiere Navale dell'Argentario's latest restoration in June 2003, although you couldn't help but think most were there just for the free *aperitivo*. After all, Charles Sibbick doesn't have the same recognition factor as Olin Stephens, and, ironically, even in her home waters *Bona Fide* is less well known than such American giants as *Dorade* and *Stormy Weather*.

The issue came to the fore at the Régates Royales later in the year where the local hero seemed to be marginalised in favour of more impressive visitors from overseas, such as the newly restored William Fife III cutter *Moonbeam IV*. Federico was understandably peeved. 'I am surprised no one here understands the importance of *Bona Fide*,' he confided. 'She was built specially to race on the Côte d'Azur, and she has a great race record. She is also the only boat built under the God net rule that has survived. She is a piece of French history.'

Ironically, it seems the very thing that made *Bona Fide* such an outstanding success when she was first launched has now become an obstacle to her being fully appreciated on the classic circuit. She is simply too modern for her age. After all, our concept of a yacht of the 1890s has

been formed by such craft as *Partridge* and *Marigold* – deep, narrow-gutted beasts that cut through the water with noble aplomb. A nimble, featherweight racer such as *Bona Fide* simply doesn't fit into our preconceived idea of what a classic yacht from that era should look like.

Yet that is exactly what makes her so fascinating. '*Bona Fide* was built in a period when the rules encouraged the fantasy of the designers. They could produce almost anything they liked within the limits of the rules. After 1907, they chopped away the craziness of the designer. Look at the fin keel on *Bona Fide* – she's like *Luna Rossa*!' said Federico, referring to the ultra-modern 2003 Italian America's Cup yacht.

Watching her distinctive, low-slung profile moving among the fleet more than 100 years after her first triumphant season on the Côte d'Azur, it's hard not to be impressed by the endurance of this most delicate-looking of craft. *Bona Fide* has already survived decades of changing fashions, and has shown she can move with the times. The only question is whether the times can move with her.

ABOVE: Built as an out-and-out racer, there is no accommodation and few home comforts on Bona Fide.

RIGHT: More than 100 years after she was launched, Sibbick's radical fin-keeler is still winning races.

What happened next...

Bona Fide won her class in the Panerai Classic Yachts Challenge in 2006 and won the Prix du Yacht de Tradition de l'Année at the Atlantic Yacht Club in 2010.

THE MASTER OF LEAN

Charles Sibbick was nearly 40 before he began designing and building boats professionally. Born in 1849, he spent the first half of his working life in the building trade, designing a few yachts as a hobby. He turned pro two years after the Yacht Racing Association adopted the Length and Sail Area Rule in 1887, giving designers the green light to play. Sibbick took over the shop at Albert Yard in Cowes on the Isle of Wight and was soon producing a steady stream of yachts.

The yard's reputation soon spread well beyond the Solent, and his designs were shipped as far afield as Hong Kong, South America, Scandinavia and the United States. Over the course of 24 years, Sibbick's yard produced more than 300 yachts to his design, nearly all of them one-offs. His most famous client was Prince George, later King George V, who ordered a 1-rater from him in 1896. Trouble was, the future monarch wanted the boat built in a week, whereas it usually took six. Sibbick nevertheless accepted the order, and set his workforce working in shifts 24 hours a day to get the yacht built in time. *White Rose* was launched five days later and two days after her launch won first prize in the Castle Yacht Club Regatta. Prince George may have walked away with the trophy, but the real winner was his doughty designer.

By the end of the 1890s, Sibbick's star was already on the wane. The rating rule had been altered and his designs were no longer so competitive. The advent of the International Rule in 1907, which encouraged more full-bodied 'wholesome' yachts, was a further setback to the master of lean. Although he attempted to diversify by building cruising yachts, it was never his passion and the yard struggled to get by. One morning in January 1912 Sibbick's rowing boat was found drifting off Cowes, empty. His body was found a few weeks later drifting in the sea nearby – a tragic end to one of yachting's most creative thinkers.

STAVANGER (1901)

THE LAST VOYAGE

'The forecast is for strong westerly wind tomorrow. The west wind comes straight from Iceland, so there will be a big sea as well.' It took a few seconds for Johan's words to sink in and for me to think: west? Straight from Iceland? Surely, he was exaggerating? But a quick look at a map confirmed it: Rørvik, where we were moored, is on the same latitude as Iceland and slightly further north than its capital city Reykjavík. Another 80 miles further north lies the Arctic Circle. No wonder it was cold!

We were sitting in *Stavanger*'s saloon, drinking coffee after a breakfast of dried cod, pickled herring and brown cheese. The wood-burning stove was lit, and the paraffin lamp was casting a warm glow over the pale oak panelling. It was a special moment not only because it was the exact same cabin where dozens of crews took shelter while performing life-saving duties during the ship's working life, but also because it was the vessel's last voyage. Ever. For *Stavanger* was a unique ship with a unique destiny. Not only was she one of the last Colin Archer rescue boats (*redningskøyte* in Norwegian) in existence, but also she was probably the most original. Owned by the same family for 59 years after being decommissioned, she was virtually as she was the day she was launched in 1901. She had no engine, no electricity, and cooking was done on a wood-burning stove.

When the Norwegian Society for Sea Rescue (NSSR) decided to buy back one of the original *redningskøyte* to be preserved for posterity, there were several Colin Archers to choose from, but *Stavanger* was at the top of their list. Less obvious was what to do with her once they'd bought her. At least half a dozen museums, each with seemingly strong claims, vied with each other to provide a home for the vessel. Eventually, the NSSR chose the Norwegian National Maritime Museum in Oslo. There, she would be exhibited close to such famous ships as *Gjøa*, the first ship to cross the North-West Passage, and *Fram*, also designed by Colin Archer and used by both Nansen and Amundsen in their polar expeditions.

It was a controversial decision, not least because the museum's intention was to lift the boat out of the water and remove a section of hull planking to give better visibility to

LEFT: This is what Stavanger *was built for: to go out to sea when other boats were heading for harbour. Her crew wears traditional gear – plus lifejackets.*

the visiting public. Which effectively meant she would never go to sea again. There were many within the Colin Archer community, and indeed the wider boating community, who argued that taking a perfectly sound boat out of service and turning her into a static display was nothing short of sacrilegious. Far better, they argued, to maintain her in sailing condition, and use her to study how an authentic *redningskøyte* performs at sea.

The argument was intensified in 1997 when, just a few months after the NSSR bought *Stavanger*, another Colin Archer rescue boat sank. *Christiania* was sailing from Norway to Denmark in a force 9 gale when she 'fell off' a wave and went down in 1,500 feet (500 metres) of water. The vessel, which had been owned by the Petersen family for 20 years, had recently undergone an extensive refit and was thought to be in 'as new' condition. Incredibly, the boat was eventually raised and restored and, three years later, was sailing once again. But the incident underlined how vulnerable these vessels are and how easily they could be lost — along with the maritime legacy they represent.

ABOVE: *Colin Archer overseeing work in his boatyard in Larvik, c1903. The boat in-build is a redningskøyte of the same class as* Stavanger.

Stavanger's skipper was Johan Petersen. His family owned *Christiania* and he was on board, along with his brother and some friends, when she sank. After overseeing her painstaking restoration, he was asked by the NSSR to take charge of the *Stavanger* project and became her de facto skipper. He fully supported the decision to take the vessel out of the water.

'During the restoration of *Christiania*, it became apparent there should be sources for how these boats were really built and how problems were solved – on a detailed level,' he said. 'During such a process, many questions arise about how to do things and, even though the general layout is well known, the details are often difficult to find. Later, when I got directly involved with *Stavanger*, it made sense to me that exactly this ship should be preserved and "frozen" in time as her source value is so great.'

But before *Stavanger* was 'frozen in time', there was time for one last, symbolic voyage: 1,000 miles from the Lofoten Islands, 120 miles north of the Arctic Circle, down the west coast of Norway and up the Oslofjord to her final resting place. On the way, she would visit most of the stations where the original rescue boats were once based, including the town of Titran on the island of Frøya, where she spent most of her 38 years in service. It was a voyage to raise awareness of *Stavanger* and of the work of the NSSR, both past and present – a chance for people to visit an original *redningskøyte*, and to imagine what life must have been like for the crews who lived on these boats.

SPECIFICATIONS

LOD: 47ft 1in (14.35m)

LWL: 41ft (12.50m)

Beam: 15ft 3in (4.65m)

Draft: 7ft 8in (2.35m)

Displacement: 31 tons

Sail area: 1,185sq ft (110m^2)

TOP. Stavanger *pictured in Kristiansund c1911, with portraits of her skipper and crew of the period.*

ABOVE: *The Norwegian rescue boats worked year round, come rain or snow.*

When I joined *Stavanger* in Rørvik, the ship and her crew had already been sailing for four weeks, and the snow that had been settling on her deck had receded to the mountain tops. Our plan was to sail to the outlying islands of Sør-Gjæslingan, 20 miles to the south-west. From there, it was 100 miles of open sea all the way to *Stavanger*'s one-time home of Titran — which is why the westerly wind was of concern. *Stavanger* could sail in any weather, as her history proved, but whether her crew was up for a 24-hour thrash into a westerly gale was another matter.

In the end, the weather was typically Norwegian: one minute gloriously calm and sunny, the next viciously dark and squally. We arrived at Sør-Gjæslingan at dusk as the wind was picking up to force 7, and eventually managed to pick out the channel into the harbour. Manoeuvring in an unfamiliar harbour with no engine, it was a matter of dropping the anchor at a safe distance off the jetty and then warping in, using the old cast iron capstan. Whenever possible, the crew tried to do things as they would have been done 100 years ago because, as much as anything, it was a chance to learn about how these boats were handled and why.

'If you don't have an engine as a backup, it forces you to think differently,' said Johan. 'We have learned a great deal of competence and knowledge sailing without an engine. For that reason, the ideal solution would be to preserve this boat and build an identical replica — without engine — to carry on learning about the old ways. But unfortunately there isn't the money to do that.'

Fishing in Norway in the 18th century was a dangerous occupation. As the industry became more lucrative, fishermen sailed ever further to gather their catch of fish, usually in small open boats really suitable only for coastal work. As a result, in 1846–1855, there were around 700–750 deaths at sea every year. But it wasn't until the Norwegian Society for Sea Rescue was established in 1891 that the idea of building seaworthy rescue boats to patrol the fisheries full-time gained credence. The following year, the society announced a competition to find a suitable design, with a prize of 150 NOK for the winner. Colin Archer was the eventual victor, and over the next 30 years some 32 lifeboats were built to his plans. Between them, they saved 2,500 lives 'from certain death'.

Stavanger was built in 1901 and was the third of the so-called Svolvaer class. She served for 37 years in the NSSR, during which time she went to the assistance of some 2,996 vessels and saved 53 lives. She earned a reputation as a seakindly vessel and seems to have been looked upon with special affection by the men who sailed her. When she was eventually sold into private hands in 1938 for the sum of 6,300 NOK, the NSSR wrote a letter to the new owners wishing them luck with the ship and describing her as 'a good sailor, perhaps the best that Colin Archer ever built for us'.

Jul and Lillerut Nielsen were both experienced sailors in their own right: Jul had owned two double-enders on which he had sailed across the North Sea, while Lillerut had saved up since primary school to have her own double-ender built. After hiding their new acquisiton in the Oslofjord for the duration of the war, they undertook a minimal conversion of *Stavanger* in 1946, including fitting an engine and heads. For the next 12 years, they sailed extensively to Spain and the Caribbean, long before such voyages became the norm. Many of their adventures were written up in the national press, and for a time *Stavanger* became something of a celebrity in Norwegian sailing circles.

Tragedy struck, however, when Jul died in a boating accident during a cruise to the Mediterranean in 1958, and Lillerut was left to look after the boat and the couple's five-year-old son Jeppe on her own. It was a profound experience for the boy, who went on to become a boat surveyor and co-founded the Risør Wooden Boat Festival in 1979. When the vessel eventually came under his care, he too resisted the temptation to alter anything and sailed her again to the Caribbean in 1986–1987 largely in original condition, albeit with a new mast.

By the mid 1990s, however, the demands of looking after an old wooden boat were taking their toll, and Jeppe gave in to the gentle but persistent courtship of the NSSR. *Stavanger* was handed over in September 1997, and in 2000–2002 underwent a gradual restoration programme at Moen

RIGHT: Manoeuvring off the dock
without an engine is a tricky business.

Båtbyggeri in Risør to reverse any changes that had been made during her time as a yacht. The engine was removed, the cockpit rebuilt and, below decks, the heads was replaced by a traditional 'Little Siri' — or wooden bucket. Even the paintwork was replicated exactly as the original, thanks to a painstaking 15-page study conducted by the Norwegian Institute for Cultural Heritage Research. The work received an official stamp of approval in 2003, when Norway's National Directorate for Cultural Heritage declared *Stavanger* an historic vessel, a status granted to less than 200 boats.

Back in Sør-Gjæslingan, the promised westerly gale had set in and it became clear that *Stavanger* and her crew wouldn't be heading for Titran any time soon. Instead, they decided to go out and film a few more manoeuvres to record how the boat performed in foul weather. As an additional touch of authenticity, they abandoned their modern foul-weather gear in favour of the yellow oilskins and black wellies their forebears might have worn. No doubt there were valuable lessons to be learned by having sea water trickling down the back of your neck.

We were soon joined by *Stavanger*'s 21st-century incarnation: the 2003 state-of-the-art 'cruising lifeboat' *Harald V*. To see the two craft side by side was to witness 100 years of evolution in boat design, and it was fascinating to see how much had changed. For, while both boats sported the NSSR's distinctive livery of white hull and red rubbing strake, they could hardly have been more different. *Stavanger*'s wood, iron and steel had been replaced entirely by aluminium, and her 110m² of canvas had been replaced by 4,000hp of engine, with a corresponding increase in speed from 7 to 24.9 knots. The prices of the two vessels had a similarly other-worldly feel, with *Stavanger*'s 10,360 NOK price tag looking like spare change compared with the 30 million NOK it cost to build *Harald V*.

Watching *Stavanger* bounding across the waves from the comfort of *Harald V*'s wheelhouse, it was apparent that the fruit of 100 years of evolution was not just comfort, efficiency and speed, but also a deep respect for the sailors of the past. In the face of all that wind and sea, the little sailing ship with its crew of yellow men looked incredibly fragile and unlikely to survive the day — let alone the next 100 years. But, all too soon, our time was up and, as *Harald V* stormed off back to Rørvik at 24 knots, *Stavanger* was reduced to a smaller and smaller speck on a vast ocean. Then, she was gone. The next time I would see her would be on dry land, a long way away from this sea she has inhabited for more than 100 years. It suddenly seemed an immense, if necessary, sacrifice.

With thanks to *Bjørn Foss* whose book *From Sail to Water-jet – The History of the Norwegian Lifeboats* provided invaluable reference.

What happened next...

Plans to build a dedicated extension for *Stavanger* were abandoned in 2014 owing to escalating costs. As of spring 2015, the boat was sitting out of the water, drying out, while her fate was decided.

Ship preservation is a relatively new field, and conservationists are still coming to grips with the best methods for maintaining these complex structures out of the water. The main issues are maintaining the shape of the hull, protecting the structure from degradation and providing appropriate access for the public. Roger Knight, former Deputy Director of the National Maritime Museum in London, has been quoted as saying that, whereas a restored building will last for about 60 years, a restored ship will last for just 12 years. That is the scale of the problem.

The *Cutty Sark* is in many ways an example of how *not* to do it. When the vessel was taken out of the water and placed in a purpose-made concrete dock in Greenwich, London, in 1954, it was assumed her original structure would be strong enough to maintain its own integrity. By the 1970s, the ship was losing her shape and 31 additional frames had to be fitted. The electrochemical reaction between the timber and the iron fastenings was such that by the 1990s additional shores had to be fitted to the counter, bilges and keel. By 2006, a wholescale restoration had to be launched, funded by Lottery money — tragically interrupted by a fire in 2007.

Much of this could have been avoided had the vessel been placed under cover and if the hull had been more sympathetically supported, using wooden rather than steel shores. The restoration process was further complicated by the fact that the keel rests on a continuous concrete plinth, rather than on removable wooden blocks, making access to the underside virtually impossible.

The Norwegian National Maritime Museum has 40 years' experience preserving a variety of wooden craft up to 70 foot (21 metres) long. They planned to put *Stavanger* under cover in the Boat Hall where, according to Communications Manager Eyvind Bagle, there would be 'standard conservation precautions to ensure that drying out does not occur'. This included treating the hull with linseed oil, wetting the deck, and caulking the seams when necessary. There was no strict temperature or humidity control in the museum, he said, although the hall was heated in winter and care was taken to avoid sudden fluctuations of temperature which might lead to condensation.

As for the controversial decision to cut a 30ft x 1ft 8in (10 x 0.5m) 'viewing hole' in the bottom of *Stavanger*'s hull, Eyvind said: 'The grounds for doing it are two. Firstly, to allow for exterior oversight and inspire our visitors to board the boat. Secondly, to provide improved ventilation of the boat. The decision rests with the project group comprising members from the museum and the NSSR, after consulting with the National Directorate for Cultural Heritage.'

OPPOSITE PAGE
TOP: No reefs even in a force 5–6, though the mizzen has been lowered as a concession to the strengthening breeze.

BOTTOM: Heading into Sør-Gjæslingan. The foot of the mainsail has been raised (ie 'triced up') to slow the boat down and give better visibility for the helmsman.

THIS PAGE
RIGHT: When a line gets in a twist, it's straight up the forestay, without a bosun's chair or harness. What would health and safety say?

FAR RIGHT: The compass is viewed through a porthole in the side of the cockpit.

(1902)

RETURN OF THE GIANT-SLAYER

It was the varnish that got me thinking. Not that it wasn't good enough – quite the opposite. The first thing I noticed when I went on board *Coral* was how immaculate her brightwork was, so I wasn't surprised when owner/skipper Richard Oswald told me he'd hired an Antiguan crew to strip the whole lot back and put on ten layers of varnish. But it did get me thinking, because I know how much those guys charge and I knew this wasn't a million-dollar, no-expense-spared operation. It's all very well employing the best varnishers in the world to make your boat look good, but if

ABOVE: Coral's unusual anchor roller mechanism looks crude, but it does keep the anchor clear of the hull.

LEFT: Back in her home waters of the Solent, after a 70-year absence.

you're on a budget then it's just a mad extravagance. But I needn't have worried. Not for nothing has Richard skippered yachts in the Caribbean and the Med for the best part of 30 years.

'The varnish crews in Antigua charge different prices for different people at different times,' he reassured me. 'If you go when the superyachts are there, you'll pay top dollar; wa t until the superyachts have left, and the price will change.'

And that's just the start of it. Richard isn't above sailing 500 miles to get a better deal on slipping his boat and treats the Caribbean like most people treat their High Street, popping from one island to the next to get the best price for whatever his boat needs. After all, when you've sailed across the Atlantic a dozen times, what's a few days' sailing between boatyards?

'Each island is good at different things. You buy stuff in St Martin; you do the most visible varnish in Antigua because they do the best job and finish it off in Grenada where it's cheaper; then you run down to Dominica to paint your bilges. You have to move around, and spread your money in communities that need it.'

It's an attitude which goes to the heart of how Richard runs his 112-year-old schooner – a size and type of vessel you might assume could be afforded only by wealthy business types employing a professional crew, or a charitable trust with an endless supply of volunteer labour. Richard is neither of these but runs *Coral* through a mixture of savvy and sheer hard work, topped with a crispy layer of bravado.

Interviewing Richard is a strange experience as he seems to have done more things than anyone could reasonably pack into his 50 years. His CV includes studying economics at the London School of Economics, teaching history at an international school in Ibiza, building his own 31-foot catamaran, skippering a 1949 classic 12-Metre yacht as well as 12 years chartering his own (modern) yacht in Europe and the Caribbean. For, unlike many sailors, who opt for either traditional or modern yachts and tend to be fiercely loyal to whichever camp they're in, Richard seems equally at ease in both.

'I'm a sailor first and foremost,' he says. 'I sail all boats. Wooden boats do have a bit more soul, and there is something special about being involved with them. As a history teacher, I like stories, I like things that touch you, that you can have empathy with. But at the end of the day, a boat's a boat.'

Richard stopped his transatlantic roaming for a few years to be a full-time parent, but then in spring 2011 he heard about a large classic yacht going for a song in Antigua. He was out there like a shot. The vessel in question was an 80-foot (24.4-metre) schooner designed by Fred Shepherd and built by White Bros in Southampton in 1902. She was in many ways an undiscovered gem, for while most of the grand old dames of that era have had multimillion dollar restorations in prominent boatyards and gone on to join the classic yacht circuit on either side of the Atlantic, *Coral* had managed to slip from view for nearly three-quarters of a century.

Yet *Coral* had more reason than most to be remembered, particularly in her home waters of the Solent. Built as *Banba III*, she wasn't particularly successful for the first 25 years of her life, until she was bought by Frank

SPECIFICATIONS

LOD: 80ft (24.4m)
LWL: 64ft (19.5m)
Beam: 15ft (4.6m)
Draft: 10ft (3m)
Displacement: 63 tons

ABOVE: A few of the dozens of blocks needed to operate the yacht's complex rig.

BELOW: Having several, smaller sails makes the schooner rig more manageable for a small crew.

BOTTOM: A lovingly crafted bronze boom fitting.

Chaplin, a member of the elite Royal Yacht Squadron. He entered *Coral* in the 1926 King's Cup against the likes of yachts such as *Moonbeam IV*, *Cariad* and *Hallowe'en*, and, according to a contemporary report, won 'handsomely', beating the scratch boat *Moonbeam IV* by 38 seconds. Just to prove this was no fluke, she won again in 1928, earning herself the accolade of the 'giant slayer'. The rules were then changed to exclude smaller yachts from the King's Cup and a new race, the Queen Mary's Cup, was created for vessels of her size. *Coral* came third in that race in 1932 and won it in 1934.

Her racing career was brought to an abrupt end by the advent of World War II when *Coral*, like many other yachts, donated her 25-ton lead keel to the war effort. After the war, she was laid up at Souter's yard in Cowes and turned into a houseboat. And there she lay, all but forgotten, for 40 years. It was in some ways her saving grace, as it meant she wasn't chopped about and 'improved' to reflect the changing fashions of the post-war years and instead remained mostly intact, with her panelled mahogany interior and teak cabin trunks as original – although her rig was long gone.

When she was eventually discovered and awakened from her 40-year slumber, it was by businessman Robin Reed, who had her shipped via Hamburg to South Africa, where he was based. A Dutch naval architect supervised the latter part of her eight-year restoration, including replacing most of the frames and all the planking below the waterline. It was the early 1990s and the classic boat revival was just kicking off in the northern hemisphere. Had she been restored there, the owner would probably have been advised to reinstate her original configuration. Instead, she was given a bullet-proof rebuild with a practical, but non-original, schooner rig for the extended sailing her new owner planned to do.

The planned cruise was not to be, however. On the first leg of her journey from South Africa, the yacht hit a storm and had to pull into St Helena, in the middle of the south Atlantic. It seems it was all too much for the owner, who headed home in the comfort of the Royal Mail ship *St Helena* and left the crew to sail the boat the rest of the way to the Caribbean. Six weeks after leaving Cape Town, *Coral* arrived in Antigua looking very much the worse for wear, with a broken boom, blackened varnish and a dispirited crew. Although already nominally on the market, she was put up seriously for sale and, thanks to a sharp-eyed friend, snapped up by Richard for an undisclosed sum – though we can assume it's more than the '£1 and other considerations' declared on the bill of sale.

It was a gift for Richard who had a network of contacts and the detailed local knowledge to get the boat back in shape quickly and relatively cheaply. For this wasn't going to be a chequebook restoration, dragging on for years, but a no-nonsense Caribbean job. After getting the varnish sorted by a top crew in Antigua (for a bargain $10k), he sailed the boat to Grenada, where the bulk of the work was done, including fitting a new boom, new backstays (with modern roller bearing blocks cunningly concealed in leather), and new awnings and upholstery.

With the bulk of the deck, rig and interior work done, *Coral* then headed down to Trinidad to make the most of cheap slipping facilities. There, the hull was recaulked and painted, and the stem, which was found to have worm in it, replaced. Lucifer, the old windlass which had taken a whole day to raise the anchor when the boat was leaving St Helena, was doubled up with a more efficient modern windlass and rode. The new anchoring system alone cost around £14,000.

Back in Antigua, a local seamstress converted a roll of raw silk cloth into a Bedouin-style outdoor shower, while another local craftsman made a customised ceramic sink for the owner's cabin. A watermaker was fitted and, as a final touch, Richard had an original 1920s Lymington scow shipped out from England to use as a tender.

Richard's plan was to charter the boat, initially in the Caribbean and then in the Med, and all the work was done with the idea that she would be able to 'wash her face' (ie pay her way) in the Med for three months of the year without spending a fortune on marina fees. 'It costs a fortune to moor *Coral* in the main marina in Ibiza, and it's not even a nice place,' he said. 'Everything was done to make us independent, like the anchoring system, the watermaker and the generator – so we can sit in some *calas* [cove] looking good, away from all that.'

Seven months later, having sailed 1,000 miles to Grenada and back, *Coral* was back in Antigua in time for the Antigua Classics, where she won third place in the *concours d'élégance*. She then set course across the Atlantic, back home to Cowes. It was the first time she had sailed in the Solent in nearly 80 years, and it turned out to be an emotional homecoming.

'We came up the Solent and sailed into Cowes under full sail just as the sun came up over the yardarm of the RYS. *Coral* rounded up in front of the RYC for the first time since 1935, and we dropped the sails really nicely. At last, she was back where she was in her heyday, which was always my intention from the moment I bought her. It was a fantastic moment.

'The first person to come on board was the harbourmaster, who remembered *Coral* from when she was a houseboat. She was owned by Len Souter and his wife Doll then, and the harbourmaster remembered Doll giving him ginger beer on the boat. Later, the whole Souter family came on board to have a look. One of them pointed to a bunk and said, "That's where Granny died."'

It was a few months after the *Britannia* replica was brought to Cowes and, while *Coral* may not have the recognition factor of her more famous contemporary, she had been a Cowes landmark for 40 years and was clearly remembered with great affection by all those who knew her. One old

RIGHT: What Coral *does best: provide jobs for many hands. Corporate team-building events provide an important source of income for the 112-year-old yacht.*

man Richard got talking to at Spencer's yard casually revealed a priceless nugget of information. All the old black and white pictures Richard had seen showed a dark hull, which he had assumed was black. But the old man pointed to a bin in the corner of the room and told him she had been that colour – racing green.

Which is why Richard renamed her *Coral of Cowes*, in recognition of the years she spent at the centre of British yachting.

Back home, *Coral* resumed her winning ways, clinching two gaffer trophies at the annual Round the Island Race around the Isle of Wight, before heading south to join the Med circuit at the Puig Vela Clàssica regatta in Barcelona. There, she raced against the likes of *Moonbeam III*, *Mariette* and *Mariquita* but, far from resuming her role as the 'giant-slayer', was crippled by her reduced cruising rig – to Richard's evident chagrin.

'*Coral* has the hull shape, but not the sail area. Her original gaff yawl rig with jackyard topsail had at least 50 per cent more power than her current schooner rig without jackyard topsail. You need a lot of power to get 63 tons of yacht going. The Beken of Cowes pictures from the 1920s show the boat really heeling, and that's how *Coral* likes to sail. She's fast and well behaved in 30 knots of wind, but unfortunately in the Med they cancel sailing when the wind blows over 20 knots.

'The solution is to fit a gaff jackyard topsail, a jib topsail and a massive genoa, and to pimp her up like *Mariette*. It's not what a schooner's designed for, but you need it for racing in light winds. You need the extra power.'

Yet, despite his reservations about her current rig, Richard didn't seem inclined to convert her back to her original yawl configuration. 'It would be incredible to return her to a yawl rig because then she could compete with the best on the Med circuit,' he said. 'But she's a great boat for family cruising as she is. The schooner rig is handy crossing oceans, and gives independence that way. It gives you enormous flexibility, and it's so easy to decrease power when you need to.'

A schooner rig also has the advantage of being manageable by a smaller crew, as each sail is smaller and therefore requires fewer people to handle it – something of concern to an owner/skipper paying monthly wages. With her existing rig, *Coral* could be sailed long distance by just four people, although there were enough strings to keep three times that many busy when she was in charter mode. And it was in the crew costs that Richard thought most savings are to be made. He claimed he could run *Coral* on 10 per cent what the big yachts on the Med circuit spent – and he was only partly joking.

But cutting costs was only half the equation, and Richard had to work hard to find the charters needed for *Coral* to 'wash her face'. Any illusions he might have had that the clients built up over 12 years chartering his previous (modern) yacht would neatly switch over to his new project were soon dispelled. Chartering a venerable old wooden yacht turned out to be a very different ball game – particularly when the cost of hiring the boat ranges from £10,000 per week for two to £15,000 per week for six.

Where *Coral* came into her own was on corporate team-building

BELOW: Coral's *exquisite panelled interior is nearly all original.*

BOTTOM: *She may not be able to pack in the numbers a modern yacht can, but she more than makes up for that in style.*

experience. The CEO of one company told Richard she was much better for that than a modern yacht because most of the tasks involve three people. Hoisting the mainsail, for example, needs three people on the throat halyard and three on the peak halyard. It's as if the whole boat has been created as an exercise in team-building – only it's for real. And the CEO put his money where his mouth was, booking *Coral* for two years running in the Round the Island Race.

There could be few people better qualified to run a boat like *Coral* than Richard, yet even he had been through a steep learning curve – not so much about how to sail a gaff schooner but how to keep an aged wooden structure afloat and the managerial demands that imposed. 'I haven't had time to read any books. I just do it. You don't read a book before driving a car; it's the same with a classic schooner. You go in with some knowledge and learn a whole lot more.'

Wise words from a former teacher – though I had a feeling the class wasn't over yet.

What happened next...

Coral of Cowes won the prize for fastest gaff-rigged yacht at the 2014 Antigua Classics. Richard planned to get married the following year.

YEAR BY YEAR

1902
Built by White Bros, Southampton, for Dr MacMahon of Cork, Ireland. Named *Banba III*

1907
Sold to Sir Hugh Drummond, chairman of London & South Western Railway, and renamed *Coral*

1924
Sold to Frank Chaplin of Royal Yacht Squadron, Cowes

1926
Won King's Cup

1928
Won King's Cup again

1932
Came third in Queen's Cup

1934
Won Queen's Cup

1939
Laid up and keel cut off for war effort

1965
Bought as houseboat by Cowes boatbuilder Len Souter

1991
Bought by Robin Reed and shipped to Hamburg, then Cape Town for restoration

2011
Sailed from Cape Town to Antigua, bought by Richard Oswald

2012
Sailed from Antigua to Cowes via the Azores. Won Shamrock Challenge Trophy (first gaffer to finish) in Round the Island Race

2013
Won Shamrock Challenge Trophy & Jubilee Trophy (first big gaffer on corrected time) in Round the Island Race

RIGHT: The original results card of the 1934 Queen's Cup, which Coral *won ahead of* Altair.

Tuesday, August 7th, 1934.
ROYAL YACHT SQUADRON.
QUEEN MARY'S CUP,
Handicap for Cruising Yachts of 15 tons gross register and upwards, owned by Members of the Royal Yacht Squadron

Queen Mary's Cup.

Sail No.	NAME.	Times. First Round H. M. S.	Times. Second Round H. M. S.	Corrected Times H. M. S.	Order.
1	ALTAIR	1 23 17	3 23 54	2 56 34	2.
2	AMARYLLIS	—			
3	CORAL	1 31 21	3 41 34	2 47 34	1.
4	GOLDEN HIND	1 37 34	3 53 31	3 18 11	
6	DIANE	—			
7	ROSEMARY IV.	1 47 33	4 30 07	3 19 27	
8	MOONBEAM	—			
9	RONA	1 46 38			
10	ARMINEL	gave up [illegible]			
11	CETONIA	1 45 49	4 27 55	3 17 15	
12	THANET	1 50 54	4 36 0	3 45 20	
14	VERA MARY	1 37 17	3 53 53	2 58 33	3.
15	AVOCET	—			
23	NORADA	—			
30	CARMELA	—			
		1 47 33	4 33 50	3 36 30	

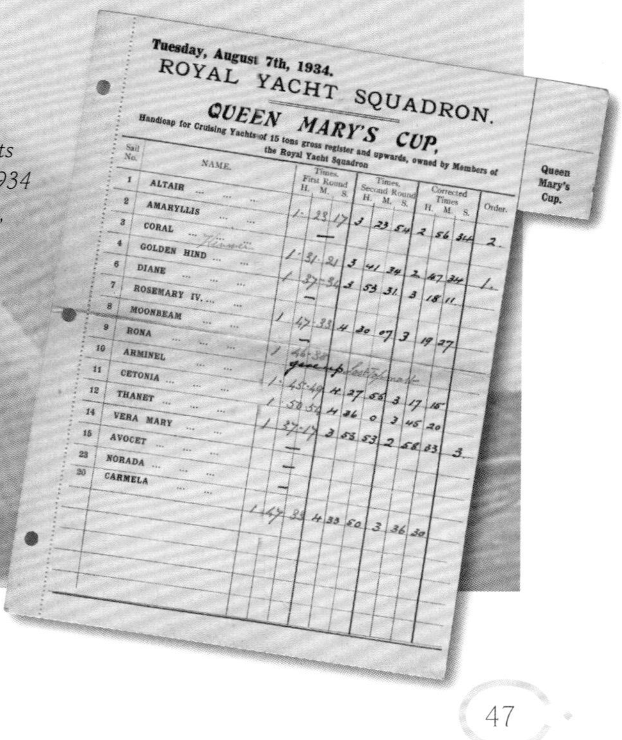

RAWENE (1908)

THE LOGAN SMILE

'She's the boat that smiles at you,' said Sandra Gorter, pointing to a shapely 42-foot (12.8-metre) gaff cutter moored off a rock just west of Auckland's Harbour Bridge. 'She's owned by Jack Gifford, who's 96 and lives in a house overlooking the harbour. Just the same as when his father had her built by the Logan brothers in 1908.'

I'd been in Auckland for three days and was looking for that special boat – one boat out of a fleet of 87 special boats – which we could feature in the next issue of *Classic Boat* magazine. My host Mark Bartlett had given me a list of suggestions, and I'd combed through the lavish colour programme with individual profiles of all the boats taking part. I'd visited half a dozen yachts on their moorings or out of the water and sailed on the outrageously curvaceous *Waitangi*.

There were so many stunningly beautiful boats to choose from, but something kept drawing me back to sail No A5. Perhaps it was the relatively understated sheer, the perfectly set counter and chirpy spoon bow. She wasn't as extreme as some of the Auckland boats, but something about her looked just right to my eye.

Rawene, it turned out, was the last major commission to be built by the legendary Logan boatyard, and was launched on Christmas Eve 1908. Two years later the yard closed and the site was leased by the Harbour Board to become the location for a power station and the King's Wharf.

The cutter was built – of triple-planked kauri – for Alf Gifford, who ran a successful tailoring business. The *New Zealand Herald* of 9 January 1909 was admiring of the new arrival: 'The fittings and finishings are of a superior kind. The woodwork of the cabin is painted white and picked out in gold, while the upholstery of the cabin is done in crimson plush. For her type she is very roomy, and looks a handsome craft afloat…'

Alf Gifford obviously thought so too. About the time *Rawene* was launched, he had a house built on the outskirts

RIGHT: Still in her original, unrestored state, Rawene *storms to victory during the 2001 Logan Classic Regatta in Auckland, New Zealand.*

TOP: Rawene *had a major refit after being hit by another boat while racing in 2005.*

CENTRE LEFT: Replacing the damaged planking.

CENTRE RIGHT: Most of the deck was renewed at the same time.

LEFT: The hull planking was as sound as the day she was built.

SPECIFICATIONS

LOA: 42ft (12.8m)
LWL: 30ft 6in (9.3m)
Beam: 8ft 6in (2.6m)
Draft: 6ft 4in (1.9m)

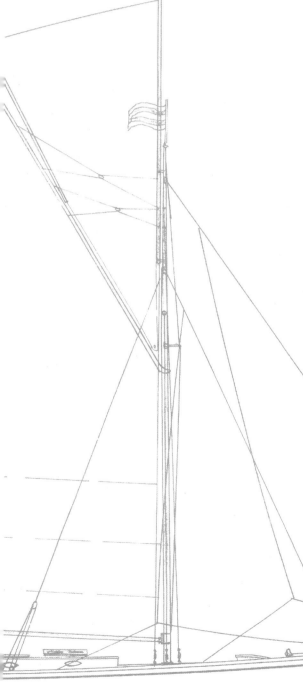

of town, with a steep terraced garden leading to a boat shed. The lawn was, of course, planted with buffalo grass – the best kind of grass to dry cotton sails on. Beyond the boat shed lay the inner reaches of the Waitemata Harbour and, about three-quarters of a mile out, Watchman Rock. It was here, a hundred yards off the rock and a five-minute row from the boatshed, that Alf had a mooring laid for *Rawene*. Thereafter, whenever the racing was over, he could sit on his veranda sipping his evening drink and admire the lines of his undeniably pretty yacht. And for the next 40 years, he did just that.

Alf wasted no time in putting his new boat to use. The day after she was launched, *Rawene* set off for a fortnight's cruise up north which, the *Herald* reported, seems to have pleased her owner: 'Mr Gifford expressed himself, at the conclusion, as being well satisfied with his boat, particularly as all sorts of weather had been encountered. The *Rawene* will compete today in the Devonport Yacht Club's cruising race, but as she is not yet in racing trim her owner does not expect her to do anything wonderful.'

How she performed in that race is not known, but there is no doubt that the boat went on to a very successful career, racing among the thriving A-Class out in the Hauraki Gulf and in particular sailing with the Royal New Zealand Yacht Squadron (RNZYS).

The yacht also seems to have been enjoyed by many of Alf's friends. Looking through the snaps of what current skipper Russell Brooke refers to as the 'cake days', the crew are dressed up in a variety of garb: hats askew, life rings around their necks, pampas grass thrust over their shoulders in mock-military fashion, and invariably huge grins on their faces. Quite clearly, these are good friends just having a great time together.

Alf continued sailing on the boat until he was in his 90s, when his son Jack took over. Aged five, Jack had broken the bottle at *Rawene*'s launching and, although rarely allowed on board during his early childhood, was eventually given the position of 'bow boy'. He was also an accomplished dinghy sailor and became commodore of the RNZYS. For some time, *Rawene* continued her winning streak – and her socialising, one of her more notable visitors during this period being the Duke of Edinburgh.

'I raced her a bit with my father in the 1950s,' Jack said. 'He could sail her better in light weather than I could, and I sailed her better in heavy weather, so we made a good team together. We took Prince Philip out during the royal visit in 1954. He came aboard and grabbed the tiller. My sister had made a very nice batch of scones and he gobbled all those up! I think he liked the way *Rawene* handled – he was quite a good sailor.'

By the end of the 1950s, however, gaff-rigged boats were becoming uncompetitive and most were upgraded to Bermudan rig. Many of Jack's sailing mates had died in the Second World War, and he had trouble finding crew. So, rather than change the vessel or watch her being gradually outclassed, he did a remarkable thing. He took off the rig, stripped the hull out and put her under cover in Westhaven, just around the corner from the family home. The boat was slipped and antifouled regularly and Jack still did much of the maintenance himself, becoming a familiar sight cycling down to tinker on the boat.

This went on for some 20 years. No doubt there were many who frowned at such a waste of a perfectly good boat, but there was another side to the story. For, while the rest of the A-Class were busily converting to pointy Bermudan rigs and having ungainly cabins added, *Rawene* remained in her original state, spending the whole of the 1960s and 70s in her own private time capsule.

And that is just how she was when the Brooke family came across her: a perfect example of Logan craftsmanship preserved in maritime aspic. The Brookes were already well known in the Auckland yachting scene. Yacht designer Jack Brooke had designed the local sail training vessel *Spirit of Adventure*, and his son Robert had been a boatbuilder for many years until a back injury forced him to take up teaching.

Robert, along with many other Auckland yachties, had been eyeing up *Rawene* for some time. But whereas others had asked to buy her, he suggested to Jack that he take on the maintenance of the boat in return for her use. This time Jack accepted – on condition the boat was kept in her original condition.

Rawene was duly re-rigged – initially with her original cotton foresails and new cotton mainsail ordered by Jack from Ratsey & Lapthorn in the UK just before the boat was mothballed – and the Wankel petrol engine was replaced with a small diesel.

The arrangement worked well for 13 years until 1992, when Robert suggested to Jack that the boat be loaned to the Auckland Maritime Museum, which was at the time collecting definitive examples of local nautical craft. As the most original Logan yacht afloat, *Rawene* was an ideal exhibit. As is often the way, however, the museum's good intentions weren't matched by its financial clout or boatbuilding know-how. *Rawene* fell into a state of disrepair and was eventually removed from the museum in 1997.

By now, Robert's three sons, Russell, Michael and Stephen, along with boating buddy Anthony Harland – who they referred to as their 'fourth brother' – were becoming keen sailors and agreed to share the maintenance of the boat. Over the next two years *Rawene* was gradually brought back up to scratch, including jobs such as stripping down and revarnishing all the spars and repairing the lead keel, which had been gouged when the boat went aground. There was also some leaking around the mast step, so part of the fore-and-aft garboard planking had to be removed and the ends of the diagonals repaired with epoxy.

It was the only use of modern materials on the boat and, when I spoke to Russell in 2001 – at which time he was education officer at the maritime museum – he was clearly sensitive to the issue of originality. 'The alternative to using epoxy would have been to take apart more of the boat and scarf in new sections of diagonals. Doing it this way, we managed to disturb the boat as little as possible.'

At that time, the interior of the boat had been freshly painted in white, although it hadn't yet been 'picked out in gold', as described by the *New Zealand Herald* in 1909. The fit-out was simple and uncluttered, and the upholstery was still 'crimson plush'. A new suit of sails had been fitted, modelled on the old cotton sails but made out of terylene.

The brothers were obviously aware of the historic value of the vessel,

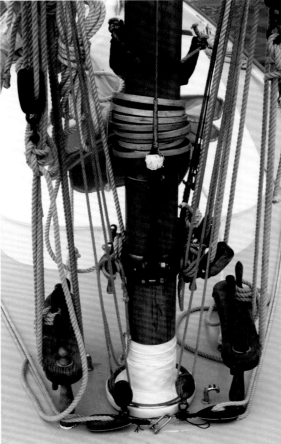

yet determined she remained in sailing, and indeed racing, condition. 'Our overriding aim is to use minimal restoration; to preserve the original artefact and keep her sailing for all to see,' said Russell. 'She can then become a reference point for future restorations of other yachts. We also sail her hard – but not stupidly, I hope! It's no good just having boats as museum pieces.'

As a final tribute to *Rawene*'s past (and to save on marina fees), the Brookes laid a new mooring off Watchman Rock and the boat was once again kept in the same spot she spent most of her early years: under the watchful gaze of the elderly man who launched her as a boy.

As we came in from a successful second race in the Logan Classic Regatta, Russell handed me the helm and we sailed under Harbour Bridge, erected long after this vessel was built, to her mooring. Up at the house, Russell immediately described the day's racing to Jack, who nodded eagerly and congratulated the brothers (all four of them). He then invited me to look at *Rawene*'s trophies, which had pride of place in his living room. Looking out from his veranda, a mature pohutukawa (the New Zealand Christmas tree) stood to one side, the bridge loomed in the distance, and there, like a perfectly composed picture, sat *Rawene* at her mooring. Jack stood beside me looking out at his boat, and when I glanced over I saw that he too was smiling.

ABOVE: Racing hard, during the 2001 Logan Classic Regatta.

TOP LEFT: Another action-packed race on Waitemata Harbour.

BOTTOM LEFT: No winches are fitted, so the sails have to be 'sweated' by hand.

What happened next...

Jack Gifford died in April 2001, soon after *Rawene* won the Logan Classic Regatta. The Brookes family continued to race the yacht, until she was sold to the Tino Rawa Trust in 2012. She is now berthed in Viaduct Harbour, in downtown Auckland.

THE LADY ANNE

(1912)

The Lady Anne won *the 2003 Fife Regatta, near her birthplace on the Clyde.*

COURTING CONTROVERSY

Getting a ride on one of these precious yachts isn't always easy, even for a journo with 'classic boat' tattooed across his forehead, as I discovered kicking around the quayside at the Régates Royales in Cannes one year.

'Of course you want to sail on her. So does everyone else. But the boss isn't bothered about getting the boat in magazines. He knows the boat's beautiful and so does everyone else. Why should he bother having you on board?'

So said a former crew of the *The Lady Anne*, a 72-foot (21.9-metre) gaff cutter which had recently been restored in the UK and was taking everyone's breath away during her second season on the Mediterranean classic yacht circuit. And he had a point. *The Lady Anne* had been star of the show at Cannes the previous year, finishing up to 33 minutes ahead of her classmate *Tuiga*, and looking supremely purposeful under her 2,465 square feet (229 square metres) of sail. Awesome was the only word to describe her. Why indeed should the owner bother humouring yet another hangdog journalist? But once on the scent I'm not easily put off, and after four days of pestering I finally got the OK from skipper Peter Mandin to join ship.

The Lady Anne was designed by the legendary Scottish designer William Fife III and built at his Fairlie yard on the Clyde in 1911–1912. She was commissioned by the wealthy yachtsman George Coats in a bid to recover the coveted 15-Metre Cup from the Germans, who had won it in 1911. At the same time as *The Lady Anne* was being built, however, Charles Nicholson was conjuring up his own design for the class, the radical 'speed machine' *Istria*. With her revolutionary Marconi gaff rig – whereby the topmast is built into the main mast, rather than 'stepped' as was traditionally the case – she would dominate the class for several years, letting *The Lady Anne* come near only in light winds. Not surprisingly, two years after launching, Coats's yacht was also converted to Marconi.

The 15-Metre class was one of ten racing yacht classes born of the first International Rule of 1907, and was by then approaching the zenith of its all too brief first incarnation. (The number '15' doesn't refer to the length of the boat, incidentally; it's just the figure produced by punching in the boat's dimensions into the formula the Rule is based on.) The mighty *Hispania* and *Tuiga*, both built in 1909, had already carved their places in yachting history, and there would be a few more years of spectacular racing before the class would be brought to a standstill by the First World War. By then, 19 of these supremely elegant yachts – 'the Maxis of their day', as yachting historian William Collier put it – had been built.

After spending the war years in Scandinavia, *The Lady Anne* raced under reduced rig in the 14-Metre class before being converted to Bermudan and racing under handicap. Like many yachts, she had her lead keel removed during the Second World War and was later spotted by William Collier in Spain in 1988, by then barely recognisable as a 15-Metre, with aluminium masts and a boxy wheelhouse. Two years later, she was up on the Hamble River, on the south coast of England, awaiting her rebirth (see panel, page 60).

Back in Cannes, *The Lady Anne* had had her propeller, propeller shaft and bracket removed before the regatta, so a tender from the owner's 'other yacht', the 207-foot (63-metre) *Adix*, towed us out to the start line. The owner's son Gonzalo and his wife Severen were on board, but the atmosphere was relaxed and friendly. The crew tended to hover amidships or at their stations, while the cockpit was the province of skipper Peter, Gonzalo, the race tactician, and Paul Goss, skipper of *Adix*, who oversaw the reconstruction of *The Lady Anne*. Severen, with all the delightful eccentricity of the habitually rich, mixed freely with the crew and peals of laughter accompanied her around the deck.

As we limbered up for the start, there was a sudden crack, and everyone looked anxiously aloft. The halyard cringle on the topsail had sheered, and a crew member was sent up the mast to check it out. Within a few minutes, the sail had been lowered, furled, and transferred to the *Adix* tender, which had brought Paul on board a few moments earlier. Another topsail was immediately set – its luff sliding up a groove in the topmast, just like the sail on a dinghy – and we manoeuvred into position for the start. The atmosphere was calm and professional; the crew had all done this a hundred times before, and it showed.

As we approached the line, nicely upwind of the rest of the fleet, *Tuiga* shadowed us to leeward. The start gun was fired, and we chased after the 1885 cutter *Partridge*, the darling of the fleet (see page 8), which had got a head start. Although we too had made a good start, a cruise ship was moored in our way, and we had to change course to tack past her bow. *Tuiga* opted to pass by the ship's stern, and by the time our paths crossed again on the other side, we were already well ahead.

The arrival of *The Lady Anne* on the scene the previous year forced *Tuiga* to up her game. For years, she had been the only 15-Metre sailing anywhere in the world, and everyone had looked on in awe at her enormous sail plan and frighteningly low topsides. With the return of her younger classmate, *Tuiga* had a direct rival and it turned out, incredibly, that if anything she was rather under-rigged. In light airs, *The Lady Anne* practically left her standing. Her 1914 Marconi rig, the second of seven rigs she sported during her long career, stood some 105 feet (32 metres) above

TOP: Sailing hard-pressed under a sudden gust of wind.

BOTTOM: The controversial mast, lined on the inside with carbon fibre, for safety.

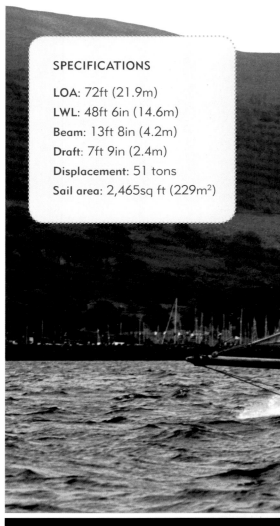

SPECIFICATIONS

LOA: 72ft (21.9m)
LWL: 48ft 6in (14.6m)
Beam: 13ft 8in (4.2m)
Draft: 7ft 9in (2.4m)
Displacement: 51 tons
Sail area: 2,465sq ft (229m²)

the water. Admittedly the newcomer's sheer wasn't quite as breathtaking as *Tuiga*'s – it was actually quite flat by comparison – but there was three years of design development between them, and *The Lady Anne* appeared to be making the most of it. The question at the beginning of each race at Cannes that year was not whether she'd come first, but by how big a margin.

But there was a bigger game at stake. Another Fife 15-Metre, *Hispania*, was being restored in the UK at that time, and the only other yacht in the class known to have survived, *Mariska*, had been tracked down to Holland. With the four surviving 15-Metre yachts all accounted for, Paul had an ambitious plan: the revival of the fleet as a racing class in its own right. 'That way, we wouldn't be bound by the penalties of CIM [the Comité International de la Meditérranée, the organisation that regulates classic yacht racing in the Med],' he said. 'And if development was allowed within the class, things could move along – and it would stop everyone bitching about their ratings. They were, after all, the development class of their age. We see ourselves on the threshold of 15-Metre racing. It's very exciting.' And, as so few of the original boats had survived, there was talk of building replica 15-Metres to race on equal terms with the restored yachts – something that would be impossible under CIM rules.

It was a seductive vision – after all, what could possibly be more beautiful than a fleet of *Tuigas* and *The Lady Annes* careering around the Med? – but I couldn't help wondering if there were other motives at play. *The Lady Anne* had come under censure from the CIM rating committee because of her 'non-conforming' spars which, although traditionally built from hollowed-out wooden sections by Harry Spencer in Cowes, were lined on the inside with carbon fibre. On this count, plus a number of other non-original items – she was fitted with a teak deck and teak cabin trunks rather than the original pine and mahogany, not to mention a microwave and other 'necessary' modern conveniences – she had been heavily penalised. The result was an allowance per mile (APM) of -39 compared with *Tuiga*'s +73, making it virtually impossible for her to win on handicap. What's more, unless she fitted new spars within the year, she risked being banned from competing in CIM races altogether.

Paul was understandably aggrieved. 'Because the yacht was going to be used for cruising as well as regattas, and possibly short-handed with guests on board, it dictated the use of carbon for safety. With modern sail cloths and synthetic lines, the rig is subjected to far higher loads than it used to be. Carbon fibre makes up only 15 per cent of the spars [the rest is wood], and is there purely to add strength rather than give stiffness or save weight. It gives minimal advantage compared with having winches, which we haven't got, especially going around the buoys.

'If you look at *The Lady Anne*, she looks completely authentic, yet we give three minutes a mile to *Tuiga*. We're here to enjoy the regatta, but we don't want to be handicapped out of it.'

The solution, Paul suggested, is to start a class of their own. But would *Tuiga* and others be expected to race against *The Lady Anne* on level terms despite the carbon fibre in her spars? 'No,' he said. 'There would be an allowance made for that, but it would be a much simpler rule.'

So how did *Tuiga* feel about that? 'It's not important,' said Bernard d'Alessandri, director general of the Monaco Yacht Club, which owned *Tuiga*. 'Carbon fibre is only 10 per cent of her performance. We enjoy racing with *The Lady Anne* with or without carbon fibre – but it would be better without.'

In fact, the competition between the two boats seemed pretty friendly. On one of my many speculative visits to try to get a place on board, I overheard Peter telling Bernard that he had been experimenting setting the flying jib very high and the staysail very low (or was it the other way around?) on downwind legs, and found it made quite a difference. 'That kind of generosity would never happen in another type of sailing,' said Bernard later.

There was something very moving about seeing these two old racehorses competing together again after all those years. We were first around the first mark, from which point we had to tack across the Golfe de Napoule to the Pointe du Cap Roux before setting off on the downwind leg. With the wind behind us, we opted to goosewing straight to the finish line, with the main on one side and an enormous genoa on the other. *Tuiga* decided to reach, hoping to get better boat speed by zigzagging down the course, and seemed to be gaining on us until she had to head off course to keep her sails filled.

It was lonely being so far out in front, and I climbed up the mast to get a better view of the fleet. I also got a close-up view of the most controversial piece of classic boat gear in the Med that season: the carbon-reinforced topmast and gaff. The carbon fibre was of course invisible, and it did seem extraordinary that this most traditional-looking of rigs could cause such a fracas, especially when even the jib sheets were tensioned using block and tackle rather than winches.

We crossed the line a comfortable eight minutes ahead of *Tuiga*, 15 minutes ahead of the 1914 Fife cutter *Moonbeam IV*, and 21 minutes ahead of the 1914 Herreshoff schooner *Mariette* – but it wasn't far enough, and on handicap we made only fourth place, behind the above-mentioned threesome. The line that really counted that day was the one I could see running between the deck and me: the mast. As long as that retained those few millimetres of magic black substance, *The Lady Anne* would not, could not win what she truly deserved. Not at Cannes, anyway. Perhaps in a revived 15-Metre class under different rules. Or might it not be simpler just to build a new set of spars?

What happened next...

After ten years away from the classic yacht circuit, *The Lady Anne* returned in 2011, with new, all-wooden spars. *Hispania* was restored in 2007, and *Mariska* in 2009. The 15-Metre Association was formed in 2012 for the four surviving 15-Metre yachts, with *The Lady Anne* winning overall in the first year. No new 15-Metres have been built to date.

THE REBUILD

As found, *The Lady Anne*'s hull was badly distorted, so new steel frames had to be lofted from plans specially created for the rebuild. New mahogany planking was then bolted to the frames, before alternate elm frames were steamed into place. Most of the deck beams were timber, except for steel ones in way of the mast.

A completely new accommodation plan was drawn, partly inspired by the interior of the 19-Metre *Mariquita*, built in 1911 at the Fife yard, which happened to be awaiting restoration at the same time. The interior was made of French walnut sourced from the Bordeaux valley. 'It's all done to a far higher standard than it would have been originally,' said project manager Paul Goss. 'Owners nowadays expect much more.'

Paul was adamant no hole should be cut into the rudder as it might cause turbulence, so the propeller shaft was offset, as Fife would have done. The propeller, shaft and bracket were all removed before racing, so her underwater shape was exactly as it was when she was launched. All the original iron deck fittings were replaced by bronze copies; only the two mainsheet bollards were original. There was nothing left of the original hull, deck, interior or rig.

ABOVE

LEFT: *The new mahogany planking was bolted to the frames and plugged.*

RIGHT: *The planks were then splined to minimise movement.*

BELOW LEFT: *A new lead keel was cast and bolted to the wooden keel.*

The Lady Anne *was banned from racing in the Med because of her 'non-conforming' spars – lined with carbon fibre.*

LULWORTH (1920)

BACK TO BASICS

'Ugly bitch' isn't a phrase you'd normally associate with a classic yacht bearing the fingerprints of the legendary designer Charles Nicholson and which saw her heyday in the Big Class in the mid 1920s. And certainly my first sight of *Lulworth*, lying in the port of Livorno in Italy, didn't seem to warrant this description. Quite the opposite. With her graceful counter stern, delightful spoon bow and effortless sheerline, she looked every bit the epitome of a gentleman's yacht. You know, the kind you see in sepia-tinted pictures, with immaculately dressed owners surrounded by legions of equally immaculately dressed crew, barely a ruffled parting in sight. The pinnacle of gentrified leisure, in other words.

Which is why I was surprised, when I got talking to the crew, to find them describing the boat in awed, if not downright fearful, terms. A few days earlier during sail trials they had achieved an impressive 16 knots in 18 knots of wind – not bad for an 86-year-old gaffer. *Lulworth* was clearly having a whale of a time and making the most of being able to sail again after a 60-year hiatus, but the crew were hanging on by the seats of their pants. 'Once the wind got above 15 knots, she turned from a beautiful woman into an ugly bitch,' said project manager Giuseppe Longo, in characteristically colourful language. 'It frightened the crap out of us. She tacks so quickly, and picks up speed in a heartbeat. We rebuilt her, but now she's showing us what to do. And we haven't even had the water over the bulwark yet!'

Later, I was told that the boat had been responsible for two deaths before she was retired from racing in 1931 – once when a spar broke and fell on one of the crew and another time in a collision during a race, although the first incident is still unconfirmed. Despite this, I clung on to my image of the yacht as a benign object of grace and beauty, in the vein of *Moonbeam IV* and *Altair*, certainly capable of respectable speed across the water but primarily to be admired for her aesthetic characteristics. That was, until I saw the yacht sailing.

After five days waiting at the quayside in Livorno, my patience was finally rewarded on the Friday as the wind eased to an acceptable force 3–4 and we headed out of the harbour. With just six crew on board (in her heyday,

LEFT: Sailing for the first time after a 60-year hiatus, Lulworth *spanks along at 12 knots off Livorno, Italy.*

she would have had 30), Cpt Gerald Read wasn't taking any chances and hoisted only the main and staysail, leaving the yacht looking slightly denuded up front. Despite this, as he eased the boat off the wind, she imperceptibly gathered pace, until she was cantering along at a steady 12 knots, leaving barely a wake behind her. It was hard to appreciate how fast she was going, until you looked at her bow. Unlike most classic yachts on the circuit, which trot along quite happily with a large 'bone' in their 'teeth', *Lulworth*'s bow sliced through the water with all the menace and efficiency of a guillotine. And, instead of the cheerful gurgle of most classics, she emitted a steady hiss, as if she had sucked the wind away from her path, leaving an eerie stillness before her.

Watching that bow, I suddenly realised that this was a very different beast indeed to the genteel cruiser/racer I had imagined her to be. I understood why she has been described by one yachting historian as a 'monstrous freak'. And I understood why, at her peak, she was one of the most successful yachts in the famous Big Class, winning a record 13 races out of 29 starts in 1926 and, famously, earning her crew more in prize money than in wages. At that moment, I felt the hairs on the back of my neck rise and I too, fleetingly, felt a brief moment of fear.

But her apparent speed isn't the only thing that's exceptional about *Lulworth*. Most obviously, there's her size. *Lulworth* is 122 feet on deck – that's 27 feet longer than the giant Fife 19-Metre *Mariquita* which wowed the classic yacht circuit after her relaunch in 2003. In fact, according to Giuseppe, the whole of *Mariquita*, bowsprit and all, would quite easily fit inside *Lulworth*. She's that big. Her waterline length is 87 feet, the same as the largest J-Class yacht ever built, *Endeavour II*, and at least 4 feet longer than any of the surviving three original 'J's. At 170ft long, her mast is thought to be the tallest wooden mast in the world, while her 5,005sqft (465m²) mainsail is said to be the largest gaff sail in the world. Her 1,430sqft (133m²) jackyard topsail alone is about the same size as the mainsail of a 12-Metre. So much for being just a gentleman's plaything.

Lulworth (ex-*Terpsichore*) was designed to the 23-Metre rule by Herbert White and built at the White Brothers boatyard in Southampton in 1920 for Richard Lee. She raced with mixed results in the Big Class until 1924, when she was bought by Herbert Weld and renamed after the family estate at Lulworth Cove in Dorset. Weld had the yacht's rig and keel profile remodelled by Charles Nicholson and the yacht soon began winning races, coming top in her class in both 1925 and 1926. With the advent of the J-Class in the 1930s, however, her star began to wane. Following the death of a crew member in a collision in 1930, *Lulworth* was retired from racing and converted for cruising. Damaged by flying debris during World War II, she was bought by Richard and Rene Lucas in 1947 and preserved by them as a houseboat on the Hamble for 43 years. So complete was the yacht at that stage that her interior was photographed and recorded by the Victoria & Albert Museum.

By 1990, however, the classic boat movement was gathering momentum, and yachts of *Lulworth*'s pedigree were becoming increasingly sought after. Rene Lucas was persuaded to part with her beloved yacht for a mere £30,000 on the understanding that she would be restored at the Beconcini

SPECIFICATIONS

LOD: 122ft (37.2m)
LWL: 87ft 3in (26.6m)
Beam: 21ft 7in (6.6m)
Draft: 18ft (5.5m)
Displacement: 189 tonnes
Sail area: 9,200sq ft (855m²)

TOP: Where the old fittings weren't available, new ones were cast in bronze.

BOTTOM: Most of the deck gear had been stored in containers, including her wheel pedestal.

OPPOSITE: The biggest gaff sail in the world? At 5,005sq ft, Lulworth's main has to be handled with caution.

ABOVE: *Several thousand feet of rope are needed to control* Lulworth's *enormous rig.*

OPPOSITE PAGE
TOP: Massive chainplates on each side of the boat are needed to hold the mast up.

CENTRE: The old cabin trunks were taken apart, cleaned up and reglued. The brass grills are original too.

BOTTOM: Period details such as the brass bell and capstan add authenticity to Lulworth's *restoration.*

yard in Italy. Instead, the yacht was gutted and much of the planking removed, but legal wrangles prevented the promised restoration from taking place and the hull was left to ossify under the Italian sun for 12 years, while the lawyers slugged it out in air-conditioned courtrooms.

Which is how Dutch entrepreneur Johan van den Bruele and his project manager Giuseppe Longo found her. 'We were at the Beconcini yard looking at other boats to restore when we saw this enormous skeleton on one side,' remembered Giuseppe. 'Most of the hull planking was missing and there was no deck, but most of the framework was still in place so you could get an idea of her shape. She looked like a beached whale. It was awesome. We didn't know anything about the boat, but we knew right away we had found something special. After five minutes Johan said, "Let's buy it."'

But the best was yet to come. Contrary to rumours that the interior had been chopped up and burned (in the way of the 1903 historic schooner *Heartsease/Adela*), it turned out that virtually every component had been carefully dismantled and stored in containers. As the elements were brought out of storage one by one, and the vessel's interior was mocked up in a shed, with cabin trunks, hatches, portholes, cleats, winches and even the original compass joining the pile, the pair realised they had reached their holy grail. If they got it right, this could be, in their words, 'the restoration of the century'.

But first they had to buy the boat. For Johan and Giuseppe were just the latest in a long line of hopeful owners who had tried to extricate the vessel from its legal quagmire. So why did they succeed when so many other, more experienced restorers had failed? 'I'm tenacious and I like a challenge,' said Giuseppe. 'In this case it was a question of being patient and finding the weak link in the chain. It took seven months of wrangling and three transactions before we got her.'

Significantly, the pair had had no previous experience of restoring a classic racing yacht. They had met on the quayside in Antibes, where Giuseppe had converted an old Feadship motorsailer into a floating youth hostel. Enamoured with the boat and impressed by Giuseppe's initiative, Johan bought *Iduna* and employed Giuseppe to restore her. The pair found a site in Viareggio where over the course of 2000–2002 the vessel was rebuilt, preserving as much of the original hull as possible but refitting the interior as a no-holds-barred luxury cruising yacht.

Johan and Giuseppe's relative lack of experience in yacht restoration was, however, to have surprising benefits when it came to tackling *Lulworth*. A property developer, Johan had restored a number of old buildings, including a 14th-century monastery in Utrecht which was sympathetically converted into a hotel. The accent in most of these projects was preservation first, replication second. It was this approach which, once they had seen how much of the original boat remained, they decided to apply to this project. 'We decided to do it the purist way just because of the fact that it was all there,' said Johan. 'Otherwise it would have been a foolish project – we may as well have built a replica. It took Giuseppe and me five minutes to decide that.'

Giuseppe concurred. 'We decided that if she was going to be a classic boat, then she would be absolutely classic. We could have put insulation behind the panelling, but I love to hear a boat creak. And we could have put bigger water tanks in, but how much is enough? How many tanks do I have to put in to reach today's standards? How low does the waterline have to get before you say, that's enough? I'm a firm believer that if an owner can have a decent shower, use a decent toilet and have a good sail, then he'll be happy.'

It's an approach which might seem like common sense to most people, but in an age where many professional restorations result in little, if any, of the original boat remaining, it attracted its fair share of criticism. 'We had someone from one well-known restoration yard come on board and tell us we should replace practically the whole lot,' said Giuseppe. 'These steps,' he said pointing at the perfectly serviceable if slightly stained main stairway, 'this panelling – the whole lot. Anything with more than two marks should be replaced, he told us. But that's like throwing away the whole spirit of the boat!' As a case in point, Giuseppe shows me a gash in the saloon panelling, which he was told should be replaced. 'But I looked at pictures from the 1920s, and that mark is in those pictures. It's part of the history of the boat – why would we want to remove it?'

Indeed, according to Giuseppe, they found plans for the reconstruction drawn by one prominent designer which, had they been implemented, would have made it impossible to reuse any of the original interior. 'Whereas the original cabin sole is stepped and angled according to the shape of the boat, these plans showed it as a straight line, which means that none of the old panels would have fitted,' he said. In one stroke of the CAD cursor, 86 years of history and a V&A-recorded interior would have been irretrievably lost.

Instead, every piece of the boat was carefully dismantled, cleaned and, wherever possible, put back together and returned to its rightful place. It was painstaking, time-consuming and, ultimately, uneconomical work, which was possible only because it was being done in Johan and Giuseppe's private yard, and not by a commercial yard working to a contract and a price.

'You see that lazarette hatch?' Giuseppe said, his eyes fiery with conviction. 'Those are the original coamings, which have been battered and knocked hundreds of times by crew dragging stuff in and out of there. It might look a mess to some people and should be replaced, but it's exactly as we found it. All we did was take it apart, clean it and stick it back together. It took probably twice as long to do as making a new one, but it's the real thing.'

Giuseppe was buzzing with excitement as he took me around the deck. 'You see that cabin trunk? It's original. We had to replace the top of that hatch because it was damaged, but the rest is original. Those halyard cleats? Original. Those deck cleats? Almost all original except for a couple which we replaced with near-replicas. We even found all the original brass hatch grills, which would have been a nightmare to make from scratch. They look a bit battered, but who cares?'

And so it went on. Giuseppe and his team even chose to make a replacement stock for the old anchor rather than replace the anchor entirely, and it still rests on its original wooden 'pizzas', rather than on more conventional chocks. All in all, Giuseppe estimates that 80 per cent of the interior and 90 per cent of the deck fittings are original. And where replacements were needed, such as some of the silver-plated door handles, copies were handcrafted from the originals.

Once word got out that the mighty *Lulworth* was finally being restored, an astonishing amount of *Lulworth* memorabilia which had been 'vanished' over the years began to reappear. The brass binnacle, mainsail sheet buffer and boarding ladder were among the more substantial 'returns', while the ship's wheel which had decorated Harry Spencer's office in Cowes was also returned to its rightful place. Even the rudder was tracked down to a scrapyard on the Hamble where it was being used as a footbridge and, although too far gone to be used, provided valuable clues for the replacement. But perhaps the nicest touch was when Neil Cozens, grandson of *Lulworth*'s first captain, Frederick Morse, donated a precious family heirloom: his grandfather's parallel rule.

It's a simplistic, almost naïve, approach, many miles away from the pragmatic and somewhat ruthless efficiency of all too many commercial yards. The closest comparison is with the 12-Metre *Vanity V* (see page 92), which was restored without a drop of glue or square inch of plywood – even down to having the replacement steel frames riveted in the style of the original, rather than applying modern welding techniques. Significantly, both projects were undertaken by relative 'outsiders' to the classic boat world, perhaps bringing with them a purism untainted by years of working in the field.

Looking at the care that has been lavished on *Lulworth*, it's impossible not to ask oneself the question: could other restorations have been done in the same way? Could we still have 80 per cent of the original interior of, for example, *Endeavour* or *Tuiga* had their restorations been approached in a different way? Of course, for those boats and many others it is too late, but it is a very real question for anyone embarking on a new restoration or, as the pool of unrestored yachts dwindles, anyone undertaking a second restoration.

'I do feel regret about the boats that were restored in the past. Especially the J-Class, which now are really just modern racing yachts,' said Johan. 'But I can't blame the people who did that. It was 20 years ago, and that was the idea then. Nowadays we are more aware. We have less of those boats around, and we know we have to look after them. I hope that, as some of these boats come up for their second restorations, they will look at *Lulworth* and understand there is another way to do it.'

What happened next…

Lulworth won the Boat International World Superyacht Awards for Best Refit in 2006. She was sold in 2010 but was back on the market in 2013, priced at €10.8m.

STEFANO FAGGIONI, INTERIOR DESIGNER

'We had a few general plans which was the base for the compartmentalisation of the boat. And we had the entire saloon and the main corridor, so they were fixed points around which we made the drawings. The only changes we made were in the owner's cabin, where we replaced a small bathroom in the back with a seating alcove and bookshelves. One of the guest cabins had already been converted into a bathroom, so we kept that and added a door into the owner's cabin to make that the owner's bathroom. And we made the guests' bathroom larger, with a shower and basin.

'Any new furniture was made in the spirit of the original – we preserved the original style absolutely religiously, so that when you open anything you have the sensation of opening an old piece of furniture. Even the hidden parts are all perfectly handmade and not commercial. We used cypress inside the wardrobes because it is a nice-smelling wood, and we want guests to remember their stay on *Lulworth* with a good smell – yes, even smell is part of the restoration!

'It was the same for the fittings. If we couldn't reuse the old ones, we made them again always remembering what was the original thought. Some of the old wall lamps were too big, so we used a section of the flower profile as a motif for the new ones. We also had to design new fridge handles, but when you touch them you should feel like you are touching something from the 1920s. The keys to the cabins were designed using the same motif as the wall lamps, so they belong to *Lulworth* and no other boat. In fact, all the fittings are unique to *Lulworth* and cannot be used anywhere else.

'The crew area was left open, so you can "read" the structure. The frames are painted white and the mahogany hull planking varnished because that is the soul of the boat and it is important to see it from the inside. The captain's cabin is made from Honduras mahogany, but painted to distinguish it from the crew and guest areas. Also, the lights in the guest area are plated with silver, in the captain's cabin they are chrome and in the crew area plain brass, to make this distinction.'

BRILLIANT (1932)

ACROSS THE AGES

Eighteen-year-old Kristen Kuczenski is browsing the internet. She clicks on the Mystic Seaport website and spots a page about a classic schooner that runs sail training trips. She has already done a day camp at Mystic, sailing dinghies, and has sailed with her aunt and uncle on board their 100-year-old catboat. But she's never done anything longer than a day trip, never sailed at night, and never sailed out of sight of land.

The schooner usually takes youngsters aged 15 to 18 on six-day trips out of Mystic, but there's a trip scheduled from Halifax, Nova Scotia, to Marblehead, Massachusetts, a distance of 350 miles. It costs $800. 'It just presented itself – it sounded perfect,' she later wrote. 'My parents were anxious and told me to be careful. But they let me go, as long as I paid for it myself. I had some money saved up from my job and decided I'd rather put it towards something than just have it sitting there. Before I left, Dad found an article on the Sydney-to-Hobart Race when loads of people died and said, "My God! Look at this!" He was really worried.'

Olin Stephens was only 22 years old when he designed *Brilliant*. Although designated design No 12, she was only the second major project for the fledgling company of Sparkman & Stephens, created by Olin, his brother Rod and Drake Sparkman in 1929. The 61-foot-5-inch (18.8-metre) schooner came after the mould-breaking yawl *Dorade* of 1930 and before the even more successful *Stormy Weather* of 1934 (see page 76), and was a very different kind of boat. Walter Barnum, who commissioned the design, was highly specific when it came to the list of specifications he handed Stephens on 2 November 1930. 'While the ship may never go around the world, she is to be designed as though that end were definitely in view,' he wrote. 'I feel we should always keep before us a mental picture of her hove-to in the middle of the North Atlantic, with the wind at 80 miles an hour and seas in proportion.'

The yacht was to be 'capable of being rolled over in a hurricane and coming up again with hull and deck opening covers intact'. Meanwhile, the rudder and steering gear were to be 'as nearly unbreakable as possible', and the hull 'as heavily timbered, planked and decked as is reasonably

LEFT: Brilliant was designed to sail around the world and be 'as nearly unsinkable as possible'. 85 years later she's still going strong.

possible'. Finally, she was to be 'as fast and weatherly as possible' and 'as handsome as possible consistent with all above'.

It was a tall order for a young designer, but Olin rose to the challenge. He combined the clean, fast hull lines he had discovered in *Dorade* with the seakeeping qualities of yachts by designers such as John Alden and Claud Worth to produce one of the most exquisite cruising yachts ever drawn. Henry B Nevins's yard in New York State built the vessel at the height of the recession for the knockdown price of $100,000 – no doubt pleased just to have the work – using the best materials at their disposal. Olin himself has described the result as 'one of the real masterpieces of wooden boatbuilding'.

And she was fast too. Twelve months after *Brilliant* was launched, Barnum sailed her across the Atlantic in a record-breaking 15 days, 1 hour and 23 minutes, and she finished fourth in that year's Fastnet Race.

After Barnum sold the yacht in 1939, she spent a few years in the Great Lakes before serving with the US Coast Guard on U-boat patrol during the Second World War. Racing car driver and yachtsman Briggs Cunningham owned her for several years after the war and funded a $75,000 refit. Eventually, Cunningham donated the vessel to Mystic Seaport in 1953, along with a commitment to fund her maintenance.

The idea was to use the yacht for sail training – a daring move at that time owing to serious doubts about whether youngsters could safely undergo training on such a large yacht. Adrian Lane was the first skipper under the vessel's new guise, running her from 1953 to 1961 and overseeing her conversion from gaff to Bermudan rig in 1958. He was followed by Biff Bowker, master until 1983, when George Moffett took over.

'She was a lot smaller than I imagined,' recalls Kristen after her first sight of Brilliant, *moored up alongside the wharf at Halifax.* 'I thought, are we really going to sail in the open sea in this little thing? I was really excited and amazed by all the clever details, like the way the table folds out. It was all so pretty, and all made of wood.

'When we motored out it was foggy, but it soon lifted and the sun was sparkling on the water. I took the helm when we hoisted sail and spent half an hour finding out how to steer her. Captain George showed me how not to overcompensate, and after that it was much easier.

'A 20- to 25-knot breeze was blowing and Brilliant *ripped down the coast towards Lunenburg under full sail, except for a single reef in the main. We heeled right over so the water was rushing past the side. At first it was kind of daunting, changing sails in that wind, but then someone showed me what to do and it was fine. It was the best sail I've ever had.*

'We stayed in Lunenburg the next day, while a front swept by out at sea. We learned some knots and polished the brass – which I like doing. You don't just learn to sail on Brilliant; *you also learn to look after her, and the line between work and enjoyment fades away.*

'We also saw the Fisheries Museum and explored the town a bit. At around sunset, we headed out to sea. Sailing at night was a new sensation. The sky was slightly overcast, and as we left the harbour the waves assaulted us with a sickening roll...'

RIGHT: Entrusted to Mystic Seaport in 1952, Brilliant *has remained unchanged ever since – even down to the sheet winches.*

BELOW: Her Wilfrid O White compass has been in continuous production for nearly 100 years.

George Moffett was lucky. He had just returned to the USA from six years running a boarding school in the UK and was looking for work in sail training when the job of mate on *Brilliant* came up. After two years getting to know the boat under his mentor Biff Bowker, he took command in 1983. By then, the yacht had settled into a comfortable routine, running 50–100-mile trips out of her base at Mystic, travelling no further than Boston to the north and New York to the south. All that was to change under Captain George.

In 1985, *Brilliant* made her first offshore trip for over 30 years when she sailed to Bermuda. The next two years, a trip to Nova Scotia was included in her programme, and in 1988 she returned to Maine for the first time in nearly 50 years, to join the annual schooner race. But her newly extended horizons also necessitated a corresponding upgrade of equipment. A new GM 353 engine was installed in 1984, and the first electronic navigation gear followed in the form of a Loran radio position finder and a single-band radio for the 1985 trip to Bermuda.

Several of the old sails ripped during that first offshore trip with trainees, and over the next few years all were gradually replaced. Incredibly, when the whole electrical system was updated in 1995, the yacht was still on her second set of batteries: a batch of Thomas Edison nickel-iron antiques.

But the biggest changes took place for the 2000 transatlantic Tall Ships Race. It was *Brilliant*'s first ocean crossing for half a century, and an opportunity to bring the yacht into the 21st century in top condition. George and the fundraising team at Mystic Seaport raised $150,000 in donations to refurbish the yacht and fund scholarships. The hull was refastened, the standing rigging was renewed (much of it still dating from 1945), a new suit of sails was fitted, a watermaker was installed, and new navigation equipment wired in, including a custom-built computer to run the Inmarsat C, weatherfax and electronic charting.

Remarkably little of the vessel's structure needed replacing. By the end of the refit, the only visible changes from the way the yacht looked in the 1930s were the liferaft on deck, the radar in the rigging and the grab rails in the saloon. It was an exceptional record for a yacht of her age.

Despite all the new equipment, *Brilliant* didn't match her record-breaking crossing of 1933, but she did well enough to come first overall in the race from Halifax to the Isle of Wight. More than 12,000 miles and 312 days later, she arrived back at Mystic Seaport having completed her longest voyage for half a century. Moffett later wrote a book about the voyage, published by Mystic Seaport Museum in 2002.

As Brilliant *leaves the shelter of land, the tail end of a storm hits the little ship. Winds of 20–25 knots on the nose force Captain George to head further out to sea, where a large swell had built up. The boat has a steady, comfortable rough-sea motion, but it's still too much for some of the trainees. Kristen is particularly badly affected.*

'I willed myself not to get seasick. But this new sensation of intense rocking and heeling proved too much – three times too much, actually. I remember thinking, if I could just get on land for one minute and get my balance back, I would be OK. But I honestly didn't want to leave or go home even when it got really bad.

'My watch ended at 2am. Our watch leader George Rockwood made me some hot chocolate to warm me up then made me go to bed to get some sleep. I don't remember much about that night except being really cold and really sick.'

The training programme on board *Brilliant* evolved while Captain George was on board. 'When I took over, I instituted a vigorous academic programme of navigation, helmsmanship, boat maintenance and seamanship,' he said. 'Then after a couple of years I realised it was more than they wanted, and that I was force-feeding them. You have to remember that for many of these kids it's just a vacation – a lot of them have never been on a boat before. We're giving them a life experience.

'People learn about the power of the sea, about being exposed to the elements, about being dependent on each other, about being a little vulnerable, about how their behaviour impacts on others – and they gain a lot more from that than learning how to tie a knot.'

Crucial in all this was the role of the watch leaders, which is where George's background in education gave him valuable insight. 'The job of the watch leaders is to give students the confidence to do things they considered impossible before. But it's tricky, because they are doing things which can hurt them badly, so it's a question of knowing when to make someone do something and when not to. It's about helping some people find their confidence, and helping other people who are cocky to guard against their cockiness.'

Thus when first-time sailor Michelle admitted she was scared of going out on the bowsprit to change the jib, she was made to do it. Every time. And by the end of the six days, she could do it with a smile – albeit clutching grimly to sail and rope. On the other hand, long-time sailor Paul, who sometimes even outsmarted Captain George on America's Cup lore, had lessons to learn about group dynamics and controlling his sometimes overbearing enthusiasm.

Brilliant arrives off Marblehead at sunrise, after two days and three nights at sea. Kristen is at the helm as the yacht weaves through the maze of lobster pots. Unnerved, she asks Captain George to take over the helm, but he refuses. Instead, he stands by and guides her quietly to the harbour entrance, after which she brings Brilliant *into the wind and drops anchor. The look on her face conveys both delight and pride. Who would have believed a week ago that she would manoeuvre 42 tons of irreplaceable vintage yacht under sail into a crowded anchorage?*

'I've learned a lot on this trip. I've got new-found respect for the sea, after the offshore passage, with a whole mixture of weather, from 25-knot winds to motoring in flat calm seas. It's been like a chocolate box of sailing experiences, and I've been able to try each one.

'Standing on land again is strange and almost dizzying, a testament to the new perspective that emerges while sailing aboard Brilliant. People tell me it will take a day or so for the world to stop swaying and return to normal, but I hope this new way of balancing will last – at least until my next sail.'

TOP: Brilliant's exquisite interior is unchanged from when she was built – apart from the addition of some discreet electronics.

BOTTOM: One of the watch leaders takes the helm, while the trainees enjoy the sunset off Nova Scotia.

What happened next...

After 24 years as skipper of *Brilliant*, George Moffett gave up his command in 2007 and made a road trip around America on motorbike. He skippered the classic ketch *Belle Aventure* for a season, before retiring in 2009. He was awarded a Lifetime's Achievement from the Mystic Seaport Museum shortly before his death, from melanoma, in 2012. He was 66. *Brilliant* continues to take young people sailing from Mystic Seaport. Applicants must be aged 15–18, fit and agile, and competent swimmers.

(1934)

SAILING WITH OLIN

It was the end of three days of racing and a small crowd was gathered on the quayside of the small town of Porto Santo Stefano, on the west coast of Italy. The judges read out the names of the winners, and the crowd applauded with varying degrees of enthusiasm, depending on the boat's popularity, the size of its crew, and the volubility of its supporters. *Mariette*, *Outlaw*, *Wild Horses* and *Cerida* all received a good response.

Then the winner of the Vintage Bermudan Yachts Over 15m was announced, and a frail old man walked unsteadily to the front. Suddenly, the crowd exploded: people cheered and clapped, cameras flashed, and even the judges wore broad smiles. The celebrated American designer Olin Stephens, from the world-famous Sparkman & Stephens company, was collecting first prize for his 1934 design *Stormy Weather*, and there was no doubt who was the most popular prizewinner on the quayside that evening.

Similar scenes took place throughout the regatta. Wherever Olin went, people lined up to talk to him and ask for his autograph. Several decades after designing his last winning America's Cup yacht (the last in a six-boat winning streak), Olin had acquired a new and unexpected following on the Mediterranean classic yacht circuit. And nowhere more so than Porto Santo Stefano, where several of his yachts had been restored to pristine condition. After attending the relaunch of *Dorade* in 1997, the dignified American gent with the crackly voice became a regular visitor to the Tuscan town, and won over everyone with his gentle clarity. By then in his mid-90s, he received the kind of recognition that all too many great people receive only after they die. But why Italy? And why then?

'The Italians have a great appreciation of classic yachts,' Olin explained. 'I think the speed of change in society means we try to find stability in grasping things that have not changed: old cars, old houses and buildings, old furniture, and so forth. Sailors who enjoy the sea for what it is – the deep pleasure of the wide horizons and the blue water – relate to boats of the period when that was not so much sacrificed for racing.'

LEFT: You can't afford to get vertigo if you're a yachting photographer; this shot was taken soon after Stormy's *restoration in 2001.*

INSET: Olin Stephens at the helm of Stormy, *aged 93.*

The focus for much of this resurgence of interest in classics was the Cantiere Navale dell' Argentario (CNA) in Porto Santo Stefano. Although established straight after the Second World War, in the mid1990s the yard developed a reputation for restoring classic yachts, thanks to a string of high-profile restorations of designs by many of the world's 'greats', including Olin Stephens, Nat Herreshoff, Charles Nicholson, Laurent Giles and Christian Jensen. *Stormy Weather* was the *cantiere*'s third Sparkman & Stephens restoration, after Olin's first major design, *Dorade*, and his 12-Metre *Nyala*. Although she had no prior links with Italy, '*Stormy*' (as she's know to her friends) was welcomed like a prodigal daughter who had finally come home.

Stormy Weather came to fame in 1935 when, a year after her launch, she won the Newport to Bergen Transatlantic Race followed by the Fastnet Race of the same year (see panel, page 83). Her success, combined with that of *Dorade* four years earlier, established Olin's reputation as a designer and cemented the burgeoning company of Sparkman & Stephens (aka S&S). The 53-foot (16.4-metre) yawl was still winning races in the mid1950s and took part in the Fastnet Race again in the 1990s. By then she was owned by the former yacht broker Paul Adamthwaite, who cruised her extensively before putting her to pasture in Canada.

The histories of the two famous S&S designs crossed again when the owner of the newly restored *Dorade* decided he needed something a little larger (a big man, he wasn't the first to find the yacht a little too narrow-gutted). Federico Nardi, CNA's managing director, knew *Stormy Weather* was for sale but considered the asking price too high. 'It was going to cost too much to restore her,' he said. 'It didn't make sense.' Instead, he suggested her sister ship, the lesser known and therefore much cheaper *Sonny*, then for sale in Maine.

It was indicative of the prestige attached to classic yachts in Italy, particularly those with a special pedigree, that *Dorade*'s owner stuck to his guns and was willing to pay over the odds for the cachet of owning the real thing. *Stormy Weather* was duly bought and shipped to Porto Santo Stefano. Although in poor condition, the yacht was sufficiently sound to sail in the 1999 Argentario Regatta, coming first in class, ahead of the newly restored *Dorade* – which, bearing in mind *Stormy Weather* was designed as an improvement of *Dorade*, seemed a fitting result.

But, while the histories of the yachts might have reconverged, life during the intervening years had treated them very differently. Whereas *Dorade* arrived at CNA needing little more than a major refit, *Stormy Weather* required a 50 per cent rebuild. Not only that, but most of what was there was not original anyway, so there was little incentive to preserve the old timber, as had been done with *Dorade* and other more unadulterated yachts. As a result, there was very little left of the original *Stormy Weather*, apart from

---

TOP LEFT: Most of the details of Stormy's *deck layout were deduced from a film made of her 1935 trip to Norway.*

CENTRE: The famous dorade vent invented by Olin Stephens's brother Rod and first fitted to their first design, Dorade.

TOP RIGHT: The winches and other deck gear were chromed during restoration at the owner's request.

RIGHT: Under spinnaker during a downwind leg of the race.

SPECIFICATIONS

LOA: 53ft 11in (16.4m)
LWL: 39ft 9in (12.1m)
Beam: 12ft 6in (3.8m)
Draft: 7ft 11in (2.4m)
Displacement: 20 tons
Sail area: 1,332sq ft (124m²)

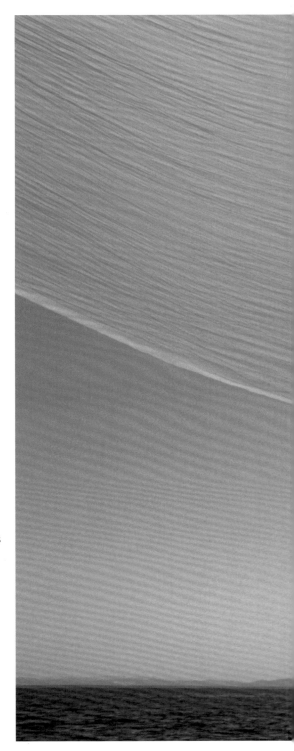

some of the underwater hull and most of the interior.

'Wherever we could, we kept the original,' said skipper Giles McLoughlin. 'But that wasn't always practical.'

Relaunch day was party day at the *cantiere*, as the spars workshop was converted into a kitchen, and bandsaws were turned into serving tables. Invites had been sent around the world, and the world's media descended on the small harbour tucked at the foot of the Tuscany hills. Well, not quite, but yours truly and a host of Italian photographers were there. The guest of honour was, of course, Olin Stephens, fresh from a symposium in his name at the Mystic Seaport maritime museum in Connecticut, USA. Also present were America's Cup designer Doug Peterson and Argentinian designer Germán Frers, who both owned classic yachts restored at the yard.

Over a *spumante* and several goat's cheese bruschettas, I asked the great man the inevitable question. Was *Stormy Weather* still his favourite design, as had oft been reported?

'I think of *Stormy* as the better of those two early successes, and she is a favourite in that sense – and as a good well-balanced design and nice fair hull,' he answered diplomatically, no doubt aware that his answer could well influence the resale price of either boat by several percentage points. 'But I prefer not to say the favourite, which would exclude later boats, such as *Intrepid* and *Running Tide*, which have claims too.'

In fact, *Stormy Weather* was barely ready in time for the relaunch. The coach roof had only one coat of white paint, and much of the interior was only semi-complete and roughly varnished. Unlike the Laurent Giles sloop *Cerida* and the 12-Metre *Nyala*, which both had immaculate new interiors built when they were restored by CNA, *Stormy Weather* retained much of her old joinery, and there were signs of patching and filling. But such is the price of originality. You have to choose between imperfect but authentic old wood, and pristine but unauthentic new wood – you can't have it both ways.

All eyes were on *Stormy* for her first appearance at the Argentario Sailing Week. Olin was on board for every race, not necessarily helming but sitting at his vigil in the cockpit. I joined them for the last day of racing, and while

BELOW: Most of the floors are made of oak, except the fore and aft ones which are bronze.

BELOW RIGHT: New ash blocks were made and sealed with a brass plate bearing the cantiere's *logo.*

LEFT: Most of the interior was non-original and was scrapped. Her near-sister ship Sonny was used as a reference point for the new interior.

ABOVE: The non-original teak-on-ply deck was also scrapped and replaced with solid teak, 27mm thick and caulked with cotton.

Olin and I waited for the crew to assemble, I asked how it felt to be on board after all those years.

'The sail balance is good,' he replied, 'but [when she comes about] she seems to want to carry on swinging, which I don't remember her doing before. No one else has noticed it, though, so maybe it's just me!' He also commented that some fittings are missing which were not on the original drawings but were added while the yacht was being built – in particular, a turning block for the jib sheets, which after the relaunch ran straight from the sail track to the winch.

The boat looked immaculate on deck – not surprisingly, as all the woodwork apart from the mast was new and had been stained an even, rich, reddy-brown colour. Most of the fittings were new too, and those that weren't had been chromed at the owner's request to match the new ones. All in all, she looked a bit like a brand-new boat, and I couldn't resist asking Olin if she still felt like she did before.

'Oh yes, she's the same boat alright,' he answered. 'I didn't sail on board *Stormy* as much as I did on *Dorade*, so I didn't get to know her as well. But apart from the steering thing, she's as I remember her.'

Skipper Giles McLoughlin, the only paid hand on board, had assembled an international crew for the regatta, including an Italian afterguard who chattered non-stop about tactics. Sandro Berti Ceroni, apparently a close friend of the owner, was on the helm and called out his commands in a deep-throated voice that made Marlon Brando's Godfather sound like a choirboy. (When I asked him later where he got his voice from, he answered simply: 'Cigarettes!')

Olin sat in the cockpit and watched everything in near silence. When he did speak, however, everyone listened. On the windward leg, an extra

tackle was attached to the mainsail boom to bring it in more line with the centre of the boat – presumably to get her to point higher, though all it did was to foul the wind for the mizzen. Olin observed it for a tack or two, and then said: 'I'm surprised that thing does any good at all.' The tackle was immediately taken off, and didn't reappear for the rest of the race.

Unlike the first two races, which took place in a gusty force 3-4, and *Stormy Weather* was fighting it out neck-and-neck with the much larger William Fife yawl *Latifa* and the Alfred Mylne cutter *The Blue Peter*, the last day was calm, with a steady force 2 blowing. The fleet was much more spread out, as sail area relative to waterline length became the deciding factor. The Herreshoff schooner *Mariette* was way out in front and, astonishingly, in second place behind her was Germán Frers's diminutive 8-Metre *Folly* (another of the *cantiere*'s recreations). She finally lost her lead on the upwind leg and Doug Peterson's 9-Metre *Tamara IX* (ditto) took the turn ahead of her, followed by *Stormy Weather*. Our handicap – a healthy +130 compared with *Tamara*'s +91 – ensured that *Stormy* won her third race in a row and clinched the series. It was a worthy return for the old lady and, as the standing ovation later that evening proved, a popular result.

Back on the quayside, several smiling Italian girls asked to have their photos taken with Olin. He looked a bit overwhelmed and, in between poses, leaned over to me and said, in a half-whisper, 'I feel like a rock star!'

'You are a rock star, Olin,' I replied. And it was true. Olin had achieved superstar status in the most unlikely of settings: a small town on the Tuscany coast, thousands of miles from his native New York. No doubt they celebrated him elsewhere too, but in Porto Santo Stefano they seemed to love him on a very personal level, as only the Italians can. No wonder he kept going back. The Americans may have bemoaned the fact that another national treasure had emigrated to the other side of the Atlantic, but there was no doubt that *Stormy Weather* had found a home somewhere she and her designer were appreciated and looked after in proper style.

ABOVE: Stormy Weather *was on winning form at the Argentario Sailing Week, 65 years after winning the Fastnet Race.*

What happened next...

After winning her class at the 2001 America's Cup Jubilee in Cowes, *Stormy Weather* was bought by British internet investor Christopher Spray. She crossed the Atlantic in 2011 and was awarded the Traditional Boat Prize for her class by the Atlantic Yacht Club. Olin Stephens died in 2008, aged 100.

Stormy Weather was built in just four months by the Henry B Nevins yard in City Island, New York, in 1934 – her designer Olin Stephens was aged 26. She got her name after her first owner, Philip LeBoutillier, heard Lena Horne performing the song 'Stormy Weather' in a nightclub shortly before the yacht was launched.

After winning both the Newport to Bergen Transatlantic Race and the Fastnet in 1935, she came first in class and second overall in the Bermuda Race the following year, finishing two minutes ahead of the Stephens-designed schooner *Brilliant* (see page 70) after nearly five days at sea. She came first in the Miami to Nassau Race five years in a row, from 1937 to 1941. And so it carried on until 1954, when she won her last major trophy, the 190-mile Storm Trysail Race.

She was then converted for charter in the Caribbean, complete with new aluminium mast, generator, and a large Mercedes diesel planted in the middle of the aft cabin. It was probably during this period, 1954–1965, that most of her original interior was lost.

She was bought in the late 1970s by Paul Adamthwaite, who undertook an extensive restoration – though, crucially, his priority was to make her fit for ocean racing rather than take her back to original. Olin's brother Rod Stephens helped with the restoration, as Adamthwaite told *Classic Boat* magazine: 'Rod was as practical as ever and used modern epoxy laminating techniques for framing and decking; stainless steel for the new mast fittings; and sails and running rigging of modern synthetics. But he was very clear that he would have used the materials employed in the 1930s had they been available.'

BLOODHOUND (1936)

A ROYAL DILEMMA

'Up there's the Queen's throne – the loo where she sat. You can try it out if you like!'

As first meetings go, it was a pretty crude introduction to one of the world's most illustrious yachts, but these words from a fellow visitor on *Bloodhound* in many ways sum up what the (former) royal yacht is all about. Spend any time on board, and it's hard to avoid the ghosts of Prince Philip and the Queen, who owned her from 1962 to 1969, and all the affiliated royals. You can't help thinking, this is the deck that the Queen trod on, this is the saloon she stood in and, yes, this is the loo where she (presumably) sat.

No wonder the relaunch of the Camper & Nicholsons yawl was greeted with such excitement by sailors and non-sailors alike, with countless articles appearing in not only the yachting press but also mainstream glossy magazines, both in the UK and abroad. Even formerly anti-royalist journalists swooned over the boat and eulogised about the sense of 'power, refinement and history' she exudes. The regal connection, it seems, carries an irresistible allure.

And yet the truth is that, although this may be the toilet that the Queen sat on, these are not the decks that she trod on and nor is this the saloon she stood in. In common with many yacht restorations, much, indeed most, of *Bloodhound*'s structure was replaced during the rebuild – including the whole interior, which had been destroyed

BELOW: *'The Queen's throne' – where HRH may or may not have sat.*

RIGHT: Bloodhound *sailing off Poole after restoration. She has since been painted navy blue.*

before this restoration even began. Not only that, but in many subtle and not-so-subtle ways she has been altered from how she was when Prince Philip sailed her. It's something that owner and project manager Tony McGrail has strong views about.

'Authenticity is a very over-debated subject,' he says. 'This will always be *Bloodhound*, even if there's only one piece of her left. In fact, we managed to keep 60 per cent of the hull structure. Below decks, we kept to the spirit of the original, although we used some artistic licence in the layout.'

Classic boat aficionados will shudder at the words 'artistic licence', as well they might. After all, this is not just any restoration project. This is a Camper & Nicholsons royal yacht. Unique and irreplaceable. Should such a priceless piece of maritime heritage be restored by a private individual with no prior experience of working on a yacht of this pedigree?

Bloodhound was designed by the famous Camper & Nicholsons boatyard in Gosport in 1936. She was the second 12-Metre built by the yard for Irish/American Isaac 'Ikey' Bell, and one of only three such yachts they ever built. Bell was a master of the hounds back home in Ireland and gave both his boats suitably hunt-orientated names. First came *Foxhound* in 1935, which he raced for less than a year before selling her to a Frenchman who made him an offer he could not refuse. He was back a year later to pick up *Bloodhound*, built to the same lines as *Foxhound*, but fitted with a rig by the legendary American designer Olin Stephens.

The C&N 12-Metres were of generally heavier scantlings than most of

SPECIFICATIONS

LOA: 63ft (19.2m)
Beam: 12ft (3.7m)
Draft: 9ft (2.8m)
Displacement: 34 tons
Sail area: 1,590sq ft (148m²)

ABOVE: Camper & Nicholsons' design was based on a 12-Metre racing yacht, but adapted for cruising.

TOP RIGHT: None of the original interior was left, so 'artistic licence' was used to create a modern layout.

BOTTOM RIGHT: These are not the decks the Queen and Prince Philip trod on – though they're probably much more watertight!

their classmates and, instead of racing with the rest of the Metre fleet, they were adapted for ocean racing and competed in Class 1 of the Royal Ocean Racing Club (RORC) divisions. *Bloodhound* soon showed her prowess, winning the Morgan Cup in her first season and ensuring a place in history by clinching a first overall in the 1939 Fastnet. Probably feeling the way the wind was blowing, Bell sold *Bloodhound* before the outbreak of the Second World War and her new owners laid her up in Gosport for the duration of hostilities. The last cannon had barely sounded, though, when she was back on the scent, claiming two firsts in the 1946 Cowes Week.

By now at the peak of her career, she was sold to someone who knew a thing or two about fast boats: Sir Miles Wyatt, Admiral of the RORC and founder of the Admiral's Cup. He was to own the yacht for 16 years and his competitive drive ensured she didn't fade away to an early retirement, like so many racing yachts of her era. Under Wyatt's tenure, *Bloodhound* added numerous more wins to her long list of accolades, including the Round the Island Race, the North Sea Race and another class first in the Fastnet. She notched up a different kind of accolade when, with Mary Blewitt installed as navigator, she won second place in the 1952 Bermuda Race, thereby becoming the first yacht in the event to employ a female navigator.

But it was not all British stiff upper lip. The yacht was very nearly lost in 1956 when, as she was leading the fleet home on the return leg of the Channel Race, hurricane-force winds hit the fleet and blew out several of her sails. Forced to abandon the race, Wyatt headed home under motor, only for the engine to break down. By then the yacht was being driven onto a dangerous lee shore off Selsey Bill, and none of the anchors they dropped were holding. Wyatt had no choice but to evacuate his crew onto a lifeboat and leave *Bloodhound* to her fate. Unbeknown to him, however, one of the yacht's anchors did get a purchase, and the boat rode out the storm on her own. The next day, the lifeboat returned to find her battered but still floating and towed her back into harbour, to the delight of her bedraggled crew.

Bloodhound's life changed for ever when, in 1962, she became the latest (though by no means youngest) member of the British royal family. Ever since learning to sail at school, Prince Philip had taken a keen interest in the sport and continued to do so as he rose through the ranks of the Royal Navy. When he married Princess (soon to be Queen) Elizabeth in 1947, one of his most prized wedding gifts was a Dragon keelboat given to the couple by the Island Sailing Club in Cowes. As well as sailing *Bluebottle* himself, Prince Philip loaned her to a number of crews, including Lt Cdr Graham Mann, who in 1958 won a bronze medal on her at the Melbourne Olympics.

By 1961, however, Prince Philip had outgrown the little yacht and was looking for something he could race offshore and take his family cruising on. Prince Charles was by then 13 years old, while Prince Andrew was just one and Prince Edward and Princess Anne had yet to be born. With the royal family growing apace, *Bluebottle*'s sailing master Lt Cdr Michael Jones was dispatched to find a suitable yacht to accommodate them all. He came up with two options: the William Fife yawl *Latifa* or *Bloodhound*, both built in the same year, albeit at opposite ends of the kingdom. Curiously, for what was one of the richest families in the world, it was the greater cost of buying and running *Latifa* that made them opt for the smaller boat in the end.

Prince Philip bought *Bloodhound* in January 1962 for £12,000, and the yacht was promptly sent back to Camper & Nicholsons for an extensive refit, overseen by that doyen of British naval architects, John Illingworth. Illingworth's own opinion of the boat was indicative: '*Bloodhound*'s sea-keeping abilities were exceptional,' he wrote to the Prince's treasurer Rear Admiral Christopher Bonham-Carter. 'Under all conditions of wind and weather she is safe and easy to handle, and going to windward she punishes herself and crew less than any boat I know.'

Despite this dazzling assessment, Illingworth instigated some major modifications. Top of the list was to replace her heavy wooden spars with new aluminium ones and, in the process, shorten the main mast to reduce the weight aloft. Sail technology had developed to such an extent since her launch that having a smaller sail area didn't necessarily mean sacrificing power. It also, conveniently, gave her a better handicap rating. The petrol engine was replaced with a 35hp Perkins diesel engine, the wooden skylights replaced with modern Perspex hatches, and the distinctive doghouse (added in the 1940s) was enlarged to include a bunk/settee. Below decks, the large owner's cabin aft was split to create two single cabins, the saloon was reconfigured and the galley and crew quarters were partitioned off to give the royals more privacy.

The alterations seem to have been effective as, two months after being relaunched in June 1962, Prince Philip sailed her at Cowes Week and, with his best friend and celebrated author/designer Uffa Fox manning the sheets, picked up a first and two second places. Not bad for a 26-year-old boat. But *Bloodhound* was nothing if not sea-kindly. 'She was easy to handle and responded very positively to her tiller,' Prince Philip later remembered. 'She was certainly much easier to steer in all conditions, with her rudder attached to her keel, than the modern round-bilged yachts with skeg rudders. Needless to say, she required quite a strong breeze to give her a chance of overcoming her handicap against smaller boats.'

When not racing, *Bloodhound* accompanied the 412-foot (125-metre) royal yacht *Britannia* on cruises, notably around the west coast of Scotland. This meant some of the family could go off and 'rough it' on what was essentially a 63-foot (19-metre) tender, while the rest could stay on the *Britannia* and be mollycoddled by her 236 crew.

But the smaller royal yacht also played another more philanthropic role. When the royal family wasn't using her, she was loaned to yacht clubs for a nominal fee for sail training. The scheme was open to any club, the only stipulation being that the guests had sufficient experience to handle the boat safely. A permanent crew of three, on loan from the Royal Navy, kept the boat running smoothly and delivered her from harbour to harbour. The clubs invited to sail were chosen depending on the royal family's cruising schedule.

The clubs scheme proved very popular and, in her first season as a royal yacht, *Bloodhound* hosted sailors from 32 clubs, sailed 6,736 nautical miles and spent 109 of her 162 days in commission at sea. The result was that, during her seven years of royal tenure, hundreds of people sailed on board the yacht and developed a deep affection for her. Sailing an ocean-going 12-Metre is always likely to be a memorable experience, but sailing a 'royal' Twelve created indelible memories for those lucky enough to experience it.

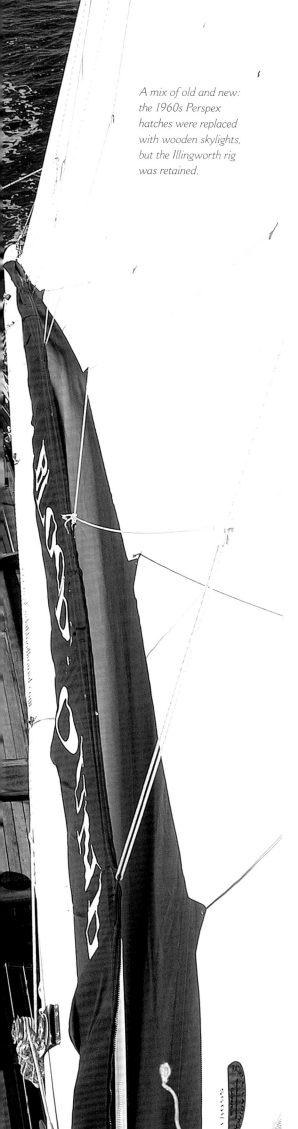

A mix of old and new: the 1960s Perspex hatches were replaced with wooden skylights, but the Illingworth rig was retained.

Long before the era of political 'spin', the *Bloodhound* clubs scheme was a PR triumph for the royal family.

By the time Prince Philip put the boat on the market in October 1969, she had sailed a remarkable 45,393 miles under his ownership. She also now had the cachet of being a 'royal yacht', and her perceived value had risen accordingly. There was, predictably, no shortage of takers and the Prince sold her within a month for £25,000 – more than double what he paid for her, proving that, when it comes to selling boats, the imprint of a royal bum in your cockpit (or heads) is worth more than any numbers of trophies on the shelf.

Bloodhound's new owner was Bernard Cook, a company director, who kept the yacht on a mooring in Poole and sailed her on the Solent until his death, when she was passed on to his son Robert. Remarkably, she stayed in the same family for over 30 years until she made her final appearance under their ownership at the America's Cup Jubilee in Cowes in 2001. Soon after, she was sold as a restoration project and taken out of the water in Poole, where she lay languishing as the new owner struggled to get to grips with the scale of the work.

A former-musician-turned-boat surveyor, Tony had heard about *Bloodhound* and seen the hull encased in scaffolding – a sure sign that work had come to a halt. By then, the interior had been ripped out and the hull shot-blasted, there were holes in the deck and some of the planking had been removed. Within a few days of seeing her, Tony had arranged the finance and put in an offer. To his surprise the owner, who by then had been courted by any number of glamorous international syndicates, accepted his offer.

Soon after, Tony moved the yacht to a barn at Sturminster Marshall in Dorset and started the restoration in earnest. It soon became clear that more work was needed than he had originally anticipated, as the decks came off completely and he was left with just the bare shell of the boat. But, as he cheerfully put it, 'In for a penny, in for a pound!'

By the time he and his small team had finished, about 60 per cent of the topside planking had been replaced, although most of the teak underwater planking was salvaged. A new teak-on-ply deck was fitted, with new wooden skylights where the Perspex hatches had been and all-new stainless steel deck fittings. The distinctive doghouse was carefully patched up and refitted, and the general deck arrangement kept as original. But this was no slavish imitation. Where it was convenient to move things, things were moved, such as the anchor winch, originally located near the mast to keep the weight of the chain as central as possible and now moved to the foredeck. There was much agonising about how this would affect the boat's trim, but Tony says that, when the 200 feet (60 metres) of chain was eventually loaded, the yacht's waterline didn't move an inch.

Below decks, there was no such compunction. As none of the original interior was left, Tony felt free to create an entirely new layout, more open-plan and user-friendly than before. The large double cabin aft was reinstated, with a pair of pilot berths added for good measure; the galley was moved aft in line with current practice, and two berths were fitted in the foc's'le. Mahogany panels and a leather upholstered sofa gave a period feel, and modern conveniences were kept to the minimum – there was no

air conditioning, watermakers or freezers, and the loos were the same old Blake heads graced by many a royal posterior.

Below decks as above, however, the standard of joinery was decidedly 2007 rather than 1936. The telltale marks of the router were all too visible, while the brightwork was lacking the patina that comes from hours of sanding between cumulative coats of varnish. It was a good enough job, but with none of the finer touches you would rightfully expect on a 1930s classic yacht.

As we set out from Poole on an idyllic summer's day, Tony displayed a refreshingly relaxed attitude to sailing. He had found and restored the yacht's original tiller during the restoration, and while at the helm he liked to adopt the same posture as Prince Philip in the old photos. As he clutched the distinctively carved tiller, there were the inevitable jokes about 'the prince's knob' and much irreverent laughter ensued. It was all good-natured fun and without any of the pomp and circumstance you might associate with a (former) royal yacht.

But Tony was no sailor and, on the single outing I went on, *Bloodhound* never achieved her true form. It was frustrating to see such a noble vessel with such an outstanding racing pedigree being effectively muzzled. Just occasionally, when the sails were set correctly and the yacht was steered in a straight line, she would find her groove. Then, for a few precious minutes, you could feel the *Bloodhound* of old, the ocean racing steed that was campaigned hard by successive owners and that won some of the toughest races in sailing. The yacht that Nicholson, Olin Stephens and Illingworth put their names to, that the admiral of the RORC raced and that under Prince Philip sailed nearly 6,000 miles per year.

The task of restoring *Bloodhound* placed an onerous responsibility on Tony's shoulders, and you have to admire him for having the guts to do it. As for whether she would have been better off in the hands of a professional boatyard, that's a question likely to divide opinion for many years to come.

ABOVE: The double berth aft was reinstated, with the addition of a pair of bunk beds.

TOP RIGHT: The distinctive doghouse was added in the 1940s but has become a feature of the boat.

What happened next...

In 2010, *Bloodhound* was bought by the Royal Yacht Britannia Trust for an undisclosed sum. When she's not berthed alongside the former royal yacht in Leith, she's based in Oban and offers day sails around the Western Isles. More info at www.royalyachtbritannia.co.uk.

THE ROYAL WARRANT

Historians are divided on which boat was the first British royal yacht. Some would have us believe it was the 30-foot (9.1-metre) coal brig *Surprise*, which whisked King Charles II off from Brighton to the safety of France in 1651. After the restoration of the monarchy in 1660, Charles bought the vessel, renamed her the *Royal Escape*, and moored her near his palace on the Thames to show her off to visitors.

The same year, however, the Dutch East India Company built a 52-foot (15.9-metre) *jacht* which was bought by the City of Amsterdam and presented to Charles as part of the so-called Dutch Gift to mark his return to power. *Mary* was richly decorated and intended purely for pleasure use, and it was on her that Charles did most of his sailing during his first year back in power. Indeed, he proved to be a keen sailor and is said to have owned 27 royal yachts between 1660 and his death in 1685.

The tradition was carried on by future monarchs, although again historians can't agree on the exact number of royal yachts that have been built, with estimates ranging from 75 to 84. The last big sailing yacht was the 325-tonne *Royal George* built for King George IV in 1817, before steam and then diesel engines became the norm.

Britannia was the last British royal yacht. Commissioned in 1954, the 360-foot (109.7-metre) vessel was designed to be converted into a naval hospital for more than 200 patients – no doubt to justify the use of public money after a time of austerity. She is said to have travelled more than a million miles and been used for 85 state visits before she was decommissioned in 1995. She is now moored in Leith, near Edinburgh, and is open to the public.

VANITY V (1936)

BEGINNER'S LUCK

Fewer than a hundred 12-Metre yachts were built from the class's inception in 1907 to the 1950s when the design was modernised. Of those vintage 'Twelves', fewer than 50 survive. So finding an unrestored pre-1950s 12-Metre, let alone one designed by the great Scottish designer William Fife, is something of a holy grail among classic yacht enthusiasts. Which is why there were a few red faces when a pair of classic car enthusiasts not only snapped one up off the quayside but proceeded to give it the kind of restoration that surpassed the best efforts of many of the so-called experts in the field.

The yacht in question was the exquisite *Vanity V*, which I joined at the fashionable sailing town of La Baule, on the west coast of France. Our destination was the Île d'Yeu, 35 nautical miles due south. After a few struggles raising the new sails in the golden morning light, we sliced across a flat sea as a moderate breeze picked up. At the helm was French Olympic yachtsman Marc Pajot, while owners Robert Daral and Jean-Paul Guillet more or less looked on as their new charge was taken through her paces.

Also on board was a man central to the whole project: yacht designer Guy Ribadeau Dumas. Guy was brought up sailing on his father's 10-Metre and as a young man always aspired to a Twelve. His brief was to ensure the restoration of *Vanity V* was completed as authentically as possible, while keeping her competitive with other 12-Metre yachts on the Mediterranean classic yacht circuit.

It was three years since Jean-Paul had spotted the yacht sitting forlornly on the quayside at St Malo. After spending years visiting the south of France, buying and selling classic wooden runabouts, he had been impressed by the growing fleet of 12-Metre yachts stealing the show at gatherings such as the Nioulargue Regatta in St Tropez, but owning one was the last thing on his mind. When he saw *Vanity V* out of the water, however, he was converted. 'I didn't know what she was,' he said. 'But I fell in love with her shape. If she had been in the water, with her modern cabin and deck, I probably wouldn't have noticed her.'

That was 1997. By the Christmas of that year, the boat had been taken to the Chantier du Guip in Brest, and a

RIGHT: As good as it gets: the inimitable lines of a true, racing 12-Metre designed by William Fife III.

few months later the restoration began. After years of restoring classic cars, speedboats and, in Robert's case, airplanes, the decision to take the boat back to as original as possible was obvious. 'It has to be a collector's piece,' said Jean-Paul. 'It has to be exactly as original, even if only 50 kilos [110lb] of it actually is original, otherwise it doesn't have the same value.'

Yard manager Yann Mauffret also saw wider significance in the project. 'This is the culmination of a movement in classic yacht restoration throughout Europe,' he said. 'We now know when we must restore a boat back to original. There are no excuses.'

For Guy, who had worked on such prestigious restorations as the 1936 Camper & Nicholsons racer *Oiseau de Feu* and the 1906 Max Oertz 10-Metre *Pesa*, it was a chance to continue his extensive research into historic yachts. 'It was twice as much work as designing a new boat,' he said. By the end of it, every deck fitting was back in its original position, the rig was returned to a 1935 configuration, and even the corners of the hatches were copied from old photos.

'The details are not given on the old plans,' Guy said. 'Fife's drawings were very succinct because the yard was just repeating what it had done many times before. So a hatch would just be a rectangle on the plans, and the builders would know what was required.' By contrast, Oertz's plans were meticulously detailed – although Guy found the standard of construction higher on *Vanity V* than on *Pesa*.

The yard's first job was to rip off the plywood deck, Perspex windows and modern superstructure, added to the boat when she was converted for cruising in the 1960s. About half the mahogany hull planking was replaced – the seams splined for ease of maintenance – and all the steel frames and floors were removed.

Rather than just weld up replacements like everyone else, however, the yard made the most of its location next to one of France's largest naval bases to take the concept of originality a step further. New Z-section frames were riveted in steel at the arsenal, just like the originals – a challenging job given the hull's compound curves, and a possible 'first' for classic boat restoration.

The new decks were laid in solid, quarter-sawn Oregon pine, doing away with the ubiquitous plywood sub-deck so beloved of most contemporary boatbuilders, although modern polysulphide sealant was used rather than traditional pitch. Guy had too many memories of pitch-stained clothing from his father's 10-Metre to espouse that particular cause. In fact, not a square inch of plywood was put into *Vanity V* during her restoration, solid timber having been used throughout.

The only original deck fitting remaining was the forward fairlead, which although well worn yielded a valuable clue. Old black-and-white photos of the boat showed her deck fittings shining brightly, which suggested that either her crew spent a lot of time polishing the brass, or her fittings were chromed. Guy guessed the latter. The forward fairlead, although verdigris bronze on top, was chromed underneath, confirming his theory.

Further research revealed that many fittings which had been made in Britain but had subsequently become unavailable there had been copied by manufacturers in Germany, where the moulds still existed. Thus, by a

SPECIFICATIONS

LOA: 70ft (21.5m)
LWL: 45ft 11in (14m)
Beam: 12ft 3in (3.74m)
Displacement: 27 tons
Sail area: 2,473sq ft (230m²)

TOP: *French racing ace Marc Pajot trims the mainsheet on* Vanity's *maiden voyage after restoration.*

ABOVE: *A chance find confirmed the deck fittings had been originally chromed.*

slight detour, it was possible to get back to the original designs. In a similar twist, *Vanity V*'s original bronze cleats had been recast in more fashionable stainless steel during the 1963 refit. It was a simple matter for the Chantier du Guip to have them recast once again in bronze to return to the original.

Below decks, the layout was mostly as the original, with a separate owner's cabin and heads aft of the midship companionway. The galley was moved aft from its 1930s position forward of the mast to allow space for the extra sails the yacht now carries. But Guy was at pains to point out that the galley has been designed so a mattress can be laid over it to replicate the old quarter berth if required.

Despite the claims of the nephew of a former owner that the interior was of cedar, Guy opted for a more luxurious mahogany fit-out. 'Considering the cost of the rest of the restoration, it was a must,' he said, in an interesting turn of logic which reveals an underlying concern, even in this most authentic of restorations, with the yacht's resale value. In the rarefied world of yacht 'collecting', mahogany is valued above cedar, even though the latter is lighter and equally durable.

But the main area where *Vanity V* departed from her adherence to originality – and therefore will never quite match the uncompromising spirit of such restorations as the 1885 cutter *Partridge* (see page 8) or the 1892 cutter *Marigold* – is in the rig. Considering that *Vanity V* lost her original mast within weeks of being launched, it's perhaps not surprising that Guy was reluctant to repeat that failure. Instead, he chose a two-spreader rig (she originally had a single spreader) from a 1935 12-Metre designed by Fife's rival, Alfred Mylne. And, although the Chantier du Guip sourced a rare log of spruce to build the hollow 39-foot-5-inch (28-metre) mast, the stainless steel rigging is decidedly modern, as are the roller bearing blocks, sliding sail tracks and shiny Meissner winches. For, while Jean-Paul and Robert wanted maximum originality, they had also specified the boat should be competitive enough to race against other, perhaps less fastidiously restored, 12-Metre yachts.

All this was of course rather academic to most of the residents of the Île d'Yeu, where we were headed. In a harbour populated on one side by a marina full of modern fibreglass yachts and on the other by a fleet of mainly wooden fishing boats, *Vanity V* made an extraordinary sight as she inched around the inner mole.

The party was soon under way. The island is famous for its tuna, and four varieties of the fish were served as an entrée, followed by langoustine for the main course and (my favourite) *tarte aux framboises* for dessert. After the meal, several of the guests took turns singing. One song concluded that the last person to give the restaurant manager's daughter a *baiser* would have to sing next, and there was a hilarious scramble to get in line to kiss her.

A few weeks later, the yacht would go off and join the rest of the 12-Metres in the posh marinas down south, and this moment would be forgotten. Yet, incongruous as *Vanity V* appeared in this modest harbour hundreds of miles from her Scottish birthplace and her historic Solent racing grounds, this was the human side of her rebirth. It was a privilege to be there to witness this very personal celebration.

BELOW: *Back on the race circuit.* Vanity V *was the 12-Metre World Champion in 2011.*

On board once again, we headed back to La Baule, which we reached in the early hours of the following morning. I wondered whether the modern compass placed in a cardboard box was some statement about originality. Yet surely yachts had compasses in the 1930s? Yes, I was told, there was a Sestrel compass, but fitting it had been delayed while they discussed whether to have it resprayed, chromed, or left as it was. In the end, they had decided to have it chromed, but it wasn't ready yet. I can't remember ever having seen a chromed Sestrel compass, but it's the kind of dilemma yacht restorers face, consider and then have to stand by their decision.

Guy has a good take on the all-excusing 'they would have used it if they'd had it then' argument: 'Vanity V is just as if she had been well maintained from original by a very conservative owner,' he said. A conservative owner with a keen sense of aesthetics shot through with a strong, yet restrained, competitive streak. Rather like the yacht's restoration team, in fact.

What happened next...

Vanity V was sold to a Danish owner and took part in the 2001 America's Cup Jubilee in Cowes. Soon after, she was sold to a British yachtsman, before returning to Danish ownership in 2006. She won the 12-Metre World Championships in 2011.

FIFE'S LAST 12-METRE

Launched in 1936, *Vanity V* was one of the last yachts built by Scottish designer William Fife III. Design No 816 never quite achieved her full potential, however, taking part in fewer than half the races she could have before the outbreak of war. At war's end, she was bought first by Sir William Shawcross and then Michael Boyle, who owned the original *Vanity*. In 1958, she was used as a trial horse for *Sceptre*'s America's Cup challenge, the defeat of which effectively spelled the end of the British 12-Metre era. Five years later, she was given a yawl rig and modern sed for cruising.

Renamed *La Pinta II*, she spent several years under the ownership of the Prouvost family, cruising to Portugal and the Mediterranean, and taking part in the early La Nioulargue classic yacht regattas in the 1990s. Gradually, however, she began to deteriorate and was taken out of the water for repairs at St Malo, where she awaited a saviour.

SOLWAY MAID (1938)

Racing in her home waters of the Clyde during the Fife Regatta.

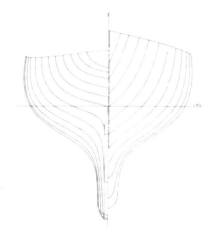

THE LAST FIFE

It was the summer of 1939 when Ivan Carr, flour miller and biscuit manufacturer, sailed up the Clyde for the last time before the outbreak of war and visited the by then world-famous yard of William Fife at Fairlie. There, he fell in love with the lines of a handsome 52-foot (15.9-metre) cruiser racer which the yard had built on spec.

'She made my mouth water,' the Carlisle businessman later wrote. 'I enquired the price, which seemed like the national debt, and went home. But could I forget her?' A few months later, war broke out and the yard, by then preoccupied with more pressing matters such as building navy pinnaces, dropped their asking price. Carr's chance had come. In October 1940, *Solway Maid*, as he named his new boat, was launched into the waters of the Clyde – the last yacht designed by William Fife to be launched at the yard.

Nearly half a century later, another boating enthusiast, Rodger Sandiford, was looking for a yacht to expand his horizons beyond his usual day sails on the Thames. He was toying with buying either a Concordia yawl or possibly even *Gipsy Moth III*, Sir Francis Chichester's original world-girdler, when he heard a rumour of an unusual boat laid up on the Clyde. The vessel was said to be an old Fife which had been mothballed at McAlister's yard in Dumbarton, unused and unaltered, for the past 14 years. Intrigued, he tracked down the owners and started negotiations. It soon transpired he wasn't the only hopeful wanting to buy the boat and yet – call it beginner's luck – a few weeks later, Rodger became the second owner of *Solway Maid*.

As the last boat to be launched at Fife's, *Solway Maid* held a special significance for lovers of wooden boats, representing as she did the culmination of two centuries of prime boatbuilding. She was also, incidentally, strikingly beautiful. Essentially a cruising version of the Metre yachts which dominated yacht racing at the time (her closest match would be a 10-Metre), she had greater beam, more accentuated sheer and higher freeboard than her racier cousins. She was also fitted with comfortable accommodation and a rig suitable for ocean passages. Historically, she was the conclusion of a line of ocean-going yachts which started with *Hallowe'en* (1926) and continued through to *Eileen* (1935), *Latifa* (1936), *Evenlode* (1937) and *Merry Dancer* (1938) – the latter two even sharing her 35-foot waterline measurement. But, although the last yacht to be launched by the Fife yard, *Solway Maid* (design No 825) was not the last to be built by them – that honour goes to *Madrigal* (design No 828) which, because she was built on commission and didn't have to wait to find an owner, was launched sooner.

But, quite apart from the 'last boat' factor, the yacht Rodger had stumbled across was special because she was so original. Not only had she kept the same owner since she was launched, but her time in mothballs corresponded exactly to the period when many old classics were being chopped up and converted to accommodate 1970s-style cruising cabins and wheelhouses. By a minor miracle, *Solway Maid* had escaped all such abuse and emerged 14 years later, unscathed, into a world that was just beginning to appreciate the value of its maritime culture. It was every collector's dream.

Aside from the quality of her build, *Solway Maid*'s remarkable condition was largely due to the meticulous care of her first owner. Ivan Carr was an experienced yachtsman when he bought the yacht and had recently completed a circumnavigation of England and Wales via the Forth and Clyde Canal on his own 35-footer. By the time *Solway Maid* was launched, however, a war was raging and he had to get special permission just to move his new acquisition the 140 miles from Fairlie to her new home of Kirkcudbright on the Solway Firth. Even then, he was allowed to do so only on condition he painted her pristine yellow pine decks grey, appended the number 'A32' on her hull and flew an enormous red ensign from her mast.

And thus began *Solway Maid*'s first period of suspended animation, as the yacht was laid up first in Kirkcudbright Harbour and then in a mud berth up the River Annan – bringing her a bit nearer to Carr's home town of Carlisle, on the other side of the border with England. It must have been a frustrating time for Carr, having just had the briefest taste of his new boat, but at least it gave him the opportunity to finish the yacht's fit-out, only partially completed by the Fife yard. It was also a chance for him to devise a number of one-off devices and systems – usually made from the stainless steel available through his work contacts at the mill – which his yacht became famous for. The foresail halyards, for example, were of fixed length and attached to quick-release hooks at the base of the mast. The mainsail halyard, on the other hand, had a dedicated windlass on deck, while its sheet was fed onto a winding drum in the cockpit. After the war, Carr also replaced the tiller with wheel steering, to save space in the cockpit.

Four years after *Solway Maid* was launched and then laid up, Carr founded and became the first commanding officer of the Carlisle Sea Cadet Corps, and his beloved yacht was finally allowed to slip her moorings – as a sail training vessel. For the rest of the war she sailed out of Silloth, on the

SPECIFICATIONS

LOA: 52ft 6in (15.9m)

LWL: 35ft (10.7m)

Beam: 10ft 10in (3.3m)

Draft: 7ft 6in (2.3m)

Displacement: 14 tons

Sail area: 1,200sq ft (111m²)

ABOVE:
The aluminium lid hides a vintage compass.

OPPOSITE PAGE
TOP: Even most of the wooden blocks are original.

BOTTOM: Solway Maid's yellow pine deck was varnished from the outset, though many sailors would consider it unseamanlike.

other side of the Solway Firth – one of the very few yachts to be allowed to sail in wartime. A few months later, with the war finally over, Carr was able to scrape the grey paint off the deck and symbolically revarnish them to their original glowing yellow. A preliminary trip to the Outer Hebrides in 1949 was followed by a cruise to Norway – one of the first British yachts to visit the country after the war.

For the next 30 years, Carr (affectionately known as 'the Skipper') sailed in the company of friends, venturing as far afield as Ireland and Brittany, but chiefly visiting the Scottish Western Isles and frequently recounting his adventures in articles in *Yachting Monthly* magazine. He was the consummate cautious skipper and caring owner. 'He was a fine seaman because he looked after his vessels,' says yachting historian Iain McAllister. 'And he never pushed his yacht to her limits: he nursed his baby, always reducing canvas prudently; rarely knowingly setting out into dirty weather. For the 34 years he owned her... *Solway Maid* was maintained and sailed with the greatest love and respect.'

After half a lifetime sailing on his beloved yacht, Carr, who suffered from a debilitating respiratory illness, died in 1974. Rather than get rid of her husband's cherished possession, however, his widow tried to preserve her memories of 'the Skipper' by having the yacht laid up at the McAlister yard. And there she languished for 14 years, apart from a brief interval in 1983 when she was launched and placed on a mooring at the Royal Northern & Clyde Yacht Club, presumably to prevent her drying out.

Around this time, Iain McAllister (no relation to the yard of almost the same name) was taking an active interest in the burgeoning classic yacht scene, and Fife yachts in particular. Living in nearby Helensburgh, he had spent much of his childhood exploring the boatyards in the area and was well aware of the hidden treasure that was lying at McAlister's. When he heard that *Solway Maid* had been bought by a South Coast yachtsman, he immediately feared the worst and contacted the new owner to inform him of the yacht's unique history and to ensure the yacht 'received the right treatment'. He need not have feared. Rodger was well aware of the significance of his acquisition and, after meeting Iain in Scotland, invited him to help bring the boat back into shape. It was a relationship that would last for 15 years.

After initial work at the McAlister yard to repair some damaged planking, in September 1988 the yacht emerged from her cocoon to sail again for the first time in 14 years and with only the second owner in her 48-year life. Rodger sailed her the following season on the Clyde, but by the end of the year it had become evident that further work was required and he took her back to McAlister's, where boatbuilder David Spy started work on her. There, under Iain's watchful eye, she received what at the time was described as a 'restoration' although, according to Iain, would by today's standards be regarded simply as a 'refit'. The alternate steel frames were derusted and treated, the fastenings replaced where necessary, the deck fittings regalvanised and rechromed and the old Gray petrol engine was replaced with a 44hp Yanmar. A new suit of cream-coloured sails was ordered from Ratsey & Lapthorn, and the extensive brightwork stripped and revarnished – including the yellow pine decks.

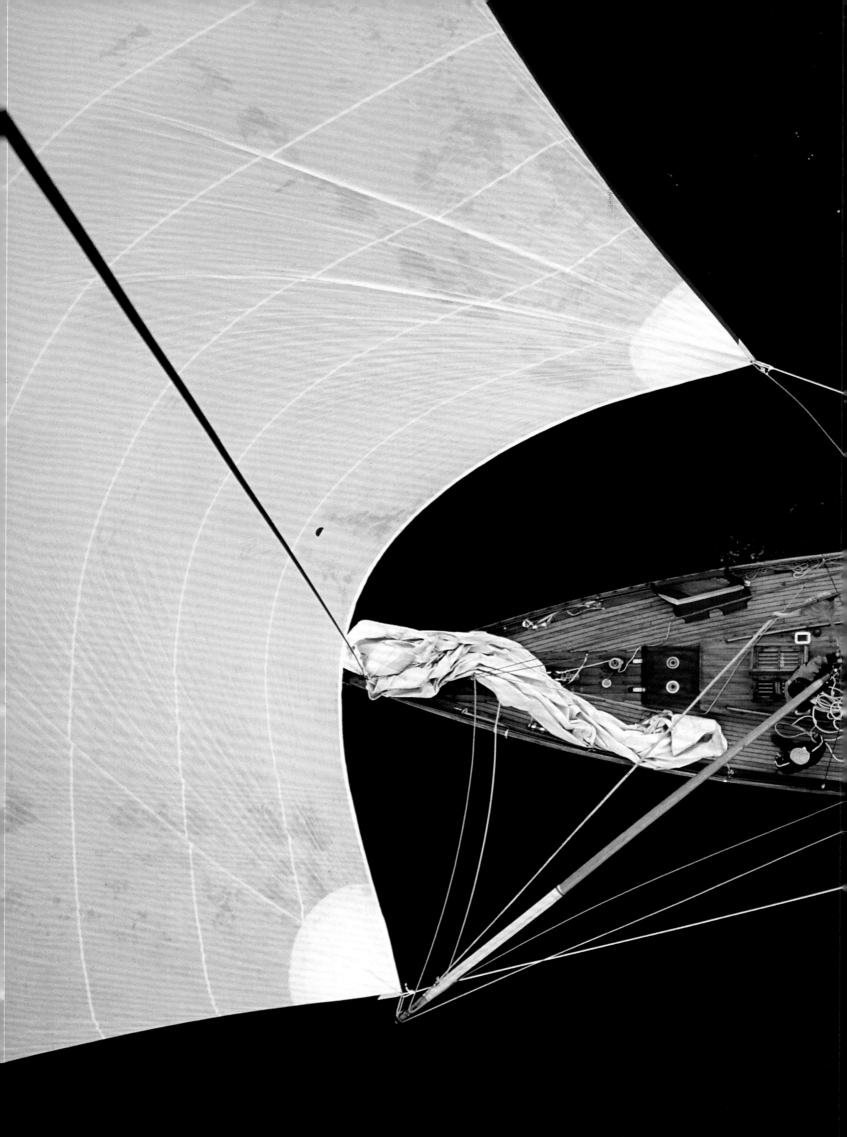

But, while the work undertaken may have been minor compared with the massive restorations (read 'rebuilds') undertaken nowadays, it was not without its challenges. 'One of the most difficult tasks was to get a sense of what was "original",' said Iain. 'Because the boat had spent all her life with one man, he had modified her as he went along and made her his own. It was something I was very aware of when I first came on the boat – it almost felt like I was trespassing, even though Carr had been dead for 14 years! We tried to find a balance between keeping that individual character and getting back to the essence of Fife – which would have been cleaner and more understated. We were trying to find a balance between Carr and Fife.'

Some of Carr's more eccentric 'gadgets' were disposed of to achieve a more Fife-like minimalism, while others were tried for a season or two before they were found to be impractical, if not positively dangerous in unknowing hands. Others, such as the unusual halyard arrangements, were found to be quite sensible and were kept. In time, several winches were added to help her race more competitively, the galley was updated by the addition of a fridge, and an autopilot was fitted to assist on long passages.

Solway Maid's 50th birthday in 1988 was an occasion for celebration. Fully restored and yet almost entirely original – including her 68-foot (20.7-metre) spruce mast – she looked every bit as exquisite as the day Ivan Carr first saw her in Fife's yard half a century earlier. Not only that, but she was headed for one of the busiest seasons of her life. With Iain by then installed as skipper, she took part in the Scottish Series in Tarbert before cruising the West Coast of Scotland, Ireland, the south coast of England – where she was the only pre-war classic to take part in that year's Cowes Week – and, finally, holing up in Douarnenez in Brittany for the autumn, before a late season hell-for-leather passage back to the Clyde.

It was a pattern that was to be repeated over the following years, as *Solway Maid* became one of the most active yachts on the classic yacht circuit, both in the UK and in the Mediterranean. And she won her fair share of trophies, from Barcelona, to Glandore and Cowes.

It wasn't all highs, however, and one of the worst moments in Iain's life happened on the very first day of the 2001 America's Cup Jubilee in Cowes. Several yachts were dismasted in the 30-knot winds that hit the Solent that day – including *The Blue Peter*, *Havsoernen* and *Blue Leopard*. One of the most poignant casualties that day was *Solway Maid*, whose mast broke above the hounds as the crew were bringing the spinnaker down. It was particularly tragic because, after 60 years of careful handling by her two owners, *Solway Maid* still had her original spars – a rare enough feat nowadays.

Speaking about it four years later, Iain still sounded choked up. 'For the previous 12 years we had sailed her to keep the rig,' he said. 'We were always gentle on her: we always reefed down early while on passage, we changed her rigging every five years – so when it came down at Cowes it was a huge shock. It was just so unnecessary.' The famed Harry Spencer yard carried out the repair – scarfing a perfect new length of spruce into the top section of the mast – and Iain recalls someone telling him it was the first original Fife mast the yard had seen.

PREVIOUS PAGE: The culmination of 136 years of boatbuilding. Solway Maid was the last yacht to be launched by the Fife yard in Fairlie, on the River Clyde (where this photo was taken).

RIGHT: She joined the Mediterranean classic yacht circuit, where she was damaged by a ferry in 2011.

Such is the weight of responsibility for anyone taking on a unique piece of cultural heritage. And yet, when I joined the boat at the four-yearly Fife Regatta in Scotland with Rodger at the helm, there was no sense of a boat being mollycoddled. Her skipper ensured the crew cranked the boat up nicely and, while she didn't win any prizes on that occasion, she was at least being raced competitively. Which is just as it should be. For while 'the Skipper' may be fretting over his baby from his heavenly perch, you can be sure that Fife himself will be willing her on to win the next race. If both of them are on the edges of their seats up in the sky, then that means the Carr–Fife balance has been achieved – and that's something that all concerned can feel justly proud of.

Additional research by Iain McAllister.

What happened next...

After a collision with a ferry off St Tropez, *Solway Maid* was given a major overhaul in 2011–2012, including replacing her coach roof. She remains the most original Fife yacht in existence.

FANEROMENI (1945)

THE TRUTH REVEALED

The late 1980s were a formative time for the classic boat movement across much of Europe. The first Douarnenez Festival took place in 1986, soon leading to the giant festivals at Brest, and the following year the 120-foot Fife schooner *Altair* was launched in Southampton after a landmark restoration. There was little such interest in old boats in Greece. There, plastic ruled the waves, and wooden boats were strictly the province of fishermen, who presumably couldn't afford anything else.

For the previous decade or so, Nikos Riginos had been riding the crest of that wave. Having sailed around North Africa on one of the new breed of yachts from the board of Dick Carter – the Carter 33, built by Olympic Marine – he went into business with his old childhood friend George Vernicos and set up Vernicos Yachts in 1975. It was one of

ABOVE: *The inside view of* Faneromeni's *distinctive feature: the Perama 'beak' which the bowsprit rests on.*

RIGHT: *A painted ship upon a painted sea...* Faneromeni *won the* concours d'élégance *at the 2014 Spetses Classic Yacht Race.*

the first companies to do serious bareboat charters in Greece – first with Carter 33s, then Olympic 38s and even a Nicholson 44, which the pair sailed down from the UK themselves. It soon branched out into yacht sales, starting with Oysters, then Jeanneaus and then Bénéteaus. The company went from strength to strength and remains one of the most successful yacht agencies in Greece.

But right in the midst of this spectacular success, Nikos did something extraordinary. In March 1987, he bought himself a wooden boat – and not just any wooden boat, but a large, old working caique, of the kind that had been built in Greece for the previous several hundred years and were the subject of long articles in respected maritime journals but which were then seriously out of fashion in Greece. The contrast between the boats he was selling and the boat he was buying could hardly have been greater.

'In those days,' says Nikos, 'caique was not a respectable word. If you said you owned a caique, you were nothing.' But Nikos, who had spent many a holiday on his father's wooden motor launch and had a natural interest in antiques, had by then had his moment of epiphany.

'When I was 15, I met Peter Throckmorton [a renowned American underwater archaeologist] and went on board his caique *Stormie Seas*,' he said. 'He was a fantastic character, and I decided at that moment that when I grew up I wanted to have a boat like that. It happened that I grew up, and it happened that I had the money to make this dream come true, and so I did!'

The Perama caique holds a special place in the pantheon of Mediterranean working boats. Unlike the more common *trehandiri* caique, which was built primarily for fishing, the Perama was a beast of burden and was bigger and more heavily built than its more nimble cousin. Its most distinctive feature is a small transom on the bow, set inside the stem, giving a strange beak-like appearance to the stem head. Theories abound as to why the Perama caique has a beak – including giving greater protection from spray, more support for the bowsprit, clearer view from the helm, or simply to facilitate planking up – but in truth no one really knows.

Throckmorton thought Perama caiques dated back to the Byzantine period and claimed they were the 'direct descendants of Roman ship types'. Either way, they made a spectacular sight plying their way across the Aegean Sea, usually under a lug or gaff schooner rig, carrying their load of watermelons, gravel or – in Throckmorton's case – compressors and diving bottles. They were also less easily converted to pleasure use and required more upkeep than a *trehandiri*, and thus soon fell by the wayside as other more practical craft took over. By the mid 1980s there were only around 20 left in active service, and this would dwindle to fewer than a dozen by the end of the century.

Faneromeni (meaning 'she who was revealed', ie the Virgin Mary) was built on the island of Skiathos in 1945. The 49-foot (13.7-metre) caique was rigged as a gaff schooner and fitted with a 30hp Kanakis auxiliary engine. She worked out of the Gulf of Volos for many years using this engine, suggesting that most of her voyaging at this time must have been done under sail, as the Kanakis would have been too small for any significant passage-making. It was her third owner, Vasilis Vallas from the

BELOW: A canine friend usually accompanies Nikos on his cruises – first Argos, then Naxos.

BOTTOM: Mastro Pachos, described by Nikos as the 'spirit of Faneromeni's *restoration', trims the coach roof beams with an adze.*

island of Kalymnos, who in 1972 finally succumbed to the inevitable and fitted a hefty 112hp Kelvin engine, presumably getting rid of her rig as he did so. The boat must still have been commercially viable, however, as Vallas owned her for many years, before eventually selling her to the nearby island of Fourni. There, she went through a succession of owners before being taken to Poros to be converted into a tourist boat.

Which was where Nikos found her. By then, her schooner rig had long gone and been replaced by a single mast supported by metal rods, of the type used for building houses, and the original deckhouse had been replaced with a large wheelhouse aft. Fortunately for him, her then owner had decided she was too small for his purposes and, after selling *Faneromeni*, went on to buy another, larger Perama caique, the *Two Brothers*, which ran tourist trips out of Poros until around 2012.

For Nikos, it was an opportunity to make his childhood dreams come true, and he proceeded with *Faneromeni*'s restoration with the same methodical approach he had applied so successfully to his work. Little information had been gathered about Perama caiques, or caiques in general, at that time, so it was a question of finding first-hand sources, such as old shipowners and boatbuilders, and looking at models and other surviving boats to find out how things had been done. Over the next few

BELOW LEFT: The 1972 Scottish-built Kelvin engine was still going strong and just needed a service.

BOTTOM LEFT: In 1992 the whole keel was replaced – an operation that Nikos says 'made my hair grow white'.

BELOW: The first thing to go was the ungainly wheelhouse, added at some point during the 1970s.

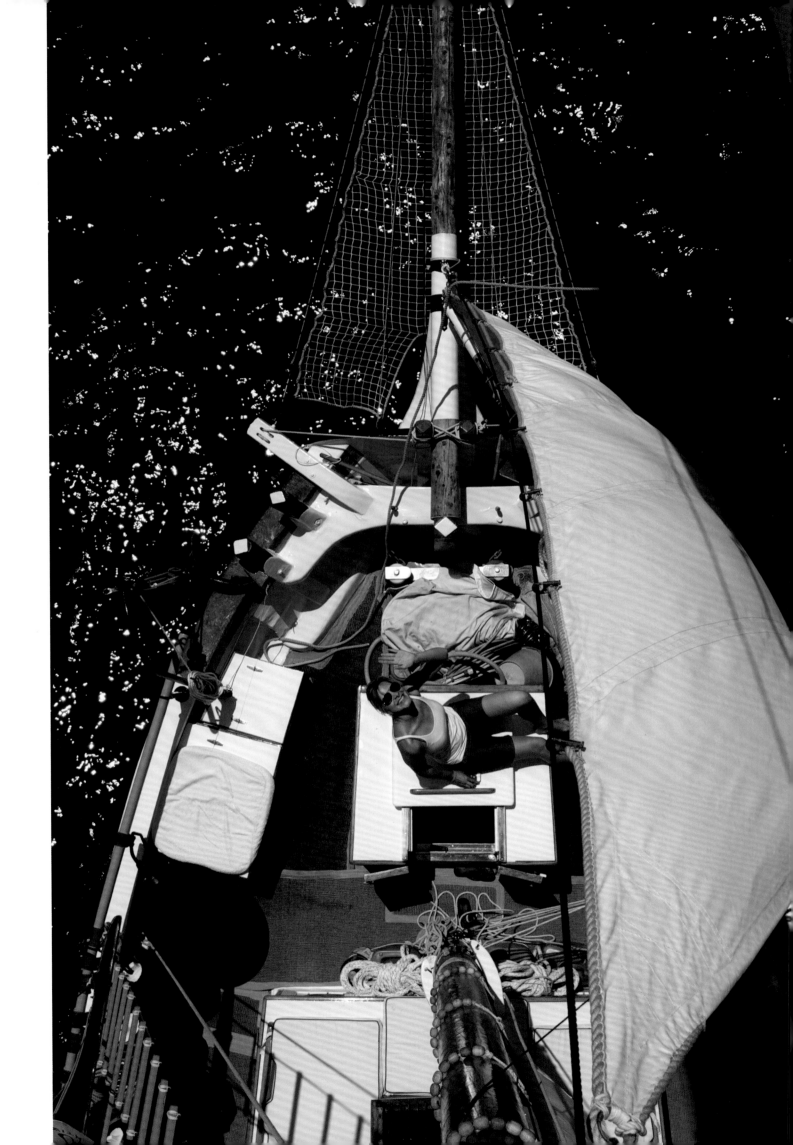

years, Nikos would travel over much of the Aegean, mostly on board *Faneromeni*, to track down all the boat's previous owners and, in the process, would become one of the foremost authorities on the subject.

Most of the restoration work took place over three years, first at the Halkitis shipyard in Perama (a suburb to the west of Pireaus) then at a marina berth in Glyfada, close to Nikos's home in the Voula suburb of Athens. The hull proved to be in surprisingly good condition and was simply burned off, recaulked and repainted, before being relaunched and taken to Glyfada. The ungainly wheelhouse had been removed, so she was more or less an empty hull and deck with an engine stuck in it. Not that a lack of amenities was going to stop Nikos taking off. No sooner than *Faneromeni* was back in the water than, in the summer of 1987, he set off with his partner Rosina for a cruise down the Saronic Gulf – the very place he had first seen Throckmorton's caique all those years before. Although *Faneromeni* was just a shell, Nikos was enthralled. In his mind's eye, he was already sailing his own *Stormie Seas*.

'Conditions aboard were primitive,' he remembered. 'We had two camp beds, which I placed in the hold. Of course there were no heads or galley – only a portable one-burner stove. For our water needs, I lashed two barrels to the mast. Refrigeration was out of the question.

'There was no windlass either, and the heavy anchor had to be raised by hand. Finally, there were not even any engine controls. Manoeuvring the boat was done like this: Rosina climbed down in the engine room and moved the engine levers according to my instructions. I would shout, "Lower the rpm," and she would immediately repeat, for verification, "Lower the rpm," and then operate the appropriate lever. I used to call her "The Engineer". Despite the primitive conditions, this was one of the nicest vacations I ever had!'

That winter, under the watchful eye of master shipwright Pachos Papastefanou (described by Nikos as the 'spirit of *Faneromeni*'s rebirth'), new deckhouses based on traditional designs were built and fitted, along with the beginnings of an airy, modern interior. New water and fuel tanks were installed, as well as a cooker, a refrigerator and even two baths with hot and cold water. An electric windlass was fitted for the anchor, and the engine even had its own controls. The Engineer could be promoted to deck – and galley – duties.

Compared with the previous summer, that year's spring cruise was luxurious. The only downside was that the boat still had no masts or sails and bobbed about 'a lot like a rowing boat'. After much searching, suitable cypress tress were found on the island of Lesbos for the spars, while the traditional waxed canvas for the sails had to be ordered from Francis Webster in Arbroath, Scotland, none being available in Greece.

Finally, in the spring of 1990, the first stage of *Faneromeni*'s restoration

TOP: The original low cabin was raised to create a comfortable doghouse for relaxation and navigation.

ABOVE: Below decks, Faneromeni's hold has been converted into a cosy saloon with adjoining galley, heads and two cabins.

OPPOSITE PAGE: The canvas for Faneromeni's sails was ordered from a mill in Scotland and the sails made on the island of Agistri.

was complete. Nikos had achieved his dream: a comfortable, fully functioning cruising Perama caique, with a schooner rig that even Peter Throckmorton would be proud of.

With the boat restored to its original sailing rig – and, in typical Nikos fashion, more immaculate than she had ever been before – he immediately set off on a series of cruises around the Aegean to significant places in her history. Despite the size of the boat, he usually sailed single-handed, or accompanied by a canine friend, first Argos and later Naxos. Around this time, he took the unusual step of retiring from his business – aged just 42 – partly so he could spend summers sailing on board *Faneromeni*.

His first stop was Skiathos, where the boat was built. Within minutes of mooring up, he was greeted by the builder's nephew, who not only remembered the boat but had actually worked on her as an apprentice. After showing Nikos the remains of the boatyard (now turned into a restaurant) he introduced him to two of the builder's sisters, who were still living in a house nearby. The women hugged him and wept when they heard the boat had returned, and Nikos spent several hours listening to stories about their brother and his yard.

'Next day, when I cast off from the harbour, I sailed the caique by their house and blew the horn as a greeting,' he remembered. 'Immediately, they came out and waved their kerchiefs and kept waving until they were no longer visible. This was another very emotional day I experienced thanks to *Faneromeni*. Even now, when I think back on it, I feel moved.'

Next up was Kalymnos, where *Faneromeni*'s third owner, Vasilis Vallas, lived. It was during his ownership that the boat was fitted with the Kelvin engine which still powers the boat to this day. After an emotional greeting, Cpt Vallas took Nikos to his home, where a hand-tinted photo hung on the living room wall. At the end of the evening, he took the picture down from the wall and, with tears in his eyes, handed it to Nikos saying, 'This now belongs to you.'

Nikos was also faced with emotional scenes when he sailed into Psara, an island north-west of Chios which *Faneromeni* delivered cargo to at one time. '*Faneromeni* had been the lifeline of the island for 20 years,' he said. 'She carried fruit, vegetables, groceries, all that was needed by the islanders. Many people gathered around. Some of them had crewed on her.'

Clearly, sailing such a historic craft is very different from sailing an anonymous modern yacht, or even a normal classic yacht. For *Faneromeni* is saturated in history in the way only a working boat that has served in a particular community can be, and sailing her in these waters will always be about much more than just sailing.

'Every boat has advantages and disadvantages – nothing's perfect,' he said. '*Faneromeni* is not a sailing yacht so you can't sail her like that, but she has other advantages: space, seaworthiness, and character. I was in a storm once when the sea flew straight from one side of the boat to the other, but she didn't flinch. She is completely trustworthy.'

Meanwhile, *Faneromeni* entered the second phase of her restoration: the never-ending one of ongoing works, familiar to any owner of old boats. First, the aft deckhouse was raised to create a proper wheelhouse, so Nikos could helm the boat in bad weather without being battered by the elements. Then a generator was installed, and the ancient Kelvin engine was completely rebuilt by the Mpekatoros brothers in Athens. Then in 2000, the bulwarks were completely rebuilt.

But the biggest job of all took place in 1992, when a yard on the island of Salamis undertook to replace the keel. Nikos was persuaded to undertake the operation partly to replace the keel bolts, which were by then dangerously corroded, and partly to improve the boat's sailing performance through the addition of an external lead keel. He regretted the decision when he saw his beloved caique suspended on props, her ribs exposed, with the keel and two adjacent planks on either side removed. The whole experience, he says, 'made my hair grow white'. But a new iroko keel was duly fitted, with one ton of lead bolted to the underside, and the boat was given a new lease of life.

In recognition of Nikos's efforts, in 1997 *Faneromeni* was declared a 'preservable monument' by the Greek Ministry of Culture, meaning that it should be preserved in its current state for perpetuity.

Since then, Nikos has cruised the boat extensively, sailing as far east as the Black Sea, and west up to Croatia. *Faneromeni* has also been a regular at the Spetses Classic Yacht Race since it was created in 2011. I joined her there and was duly impressed by the high standard of care Nikos lavishes on his charge. Nothing, it seems, is too much effort, from the custom-made adjustable fender clips to the tailored deck matting (to protect the wood from the midday sun) and the spotless engine room.

Like most cargo boats, *Faneromeni* needs a breeze to get her going, and the wind barely reached force 3 on the day I was on board. The main difficulty was keeping enough speed on to maintain steerage. We finished mid fleet in our class, a respectable result, but what was more impressive was that there were so many other caiques – including at least one other Perama – racing together under sail. For these boats are now treated like returning royalty in Greece. Indeed, the organisers of the Spetses Regatta have created a special class, the Aegean Schooners, to encourage more caiques to participate, and there's a parade of sail specially for local boats.

It's all a long way from when Nikos first spotted *Faneromeni*, when the only thing celebrated about caiques was the fish they caught or the number of sunburned tourists they could transport from beach to beach.

'When I bought her everyone thought I was mad,' says Nikos. 'Now they all say what a great boat she is. Only now we are losing our heritage, people start to value the old boats more.'

For the past 30 years, Nikos has shown how it can be done. For 30 years, he has sailed *Faneromeni* from port to port, for his own pleasure but also as an ambassador of Greek maritime culture – a culture long consigned to the dustbin by most of his compatriots. And finally, it seems, other sailors are catching up and beginning to appreciate the value of what they have so nearly thrown away. Just as Peter Throckmorton inspired him when he was a boy, so Nikos now inspires others to follow in his wake. For in *Faneromeni*, he has created a vessel which will continue the legacy of *Stormie Seas* and other vessels like her, hopefully for many generations to come.

OPPOSITE PAGE

TOP: A decorative wooden fish spreads the load of Faneromeni's bobstay.

CENTRE: Wooden blocks are used to haul the fisherman's anchor out of the water.

BOTTOM: A neat (and very modern) arrangement for adjusting the fender lines.

What happened next...

Faneromeni was winner of the *concours d'élégance* in her class at the 2014 Spetses Classic Yacht Race.

INWARD BOUND

BOOTLEG CLASSIC

At 4pm on 2 May 1982 the cruiser *General Belgrano* was sunk 100 miles off the coast of Argentina with the loss of 323 lives. The sinking of Argentina's only cruiser by the British submarine HMS *Conqueror* at the peak of the Falklands crisis sparked controversy when it was reported that not only was the ship outside the exclusion zone but she was steaming away from the conflict area. For others, however, the incident was a key factor in the UK's eventual victory, which in turn helped sweep Margaret Thatcher back to power a few months later.

But, while the *Belgrano* (formerly the USS *Phoenix*) herself sits in a watery grave 14,000ft under the sea, a small part of the infamous World War II battleship sails on (phoenix-like) 7,000 miles further north, on the waters of Lake Ontario in Canada. And we're not talking about some artefact in an obscure military museum but a very active and sometimes ocean-bound 35-foot (10.6-metre) yacht.

Inward Bound (ex-*Barracuda*) was built at the Astilleros Sarmiento yard in Buenos Aires in 1962 for a wealthy Argentinian. Although her lines appear to be those of a Pilot 35 (Design No 1219-G), a salty cruiser/racer designed by Sparkman & Stephens, her exact provenance is a mystery. There is nothing from her builder linking her to S&S and the designers themselves have no record of any Pilot 35 plans being sent out to Argentina at that time. There is a theory that a Uruguay apprentice who was working in the S&S office at that time may have taken a set of plans home with him and copied them, but that is just speculation.

What is certain is that *Inward Bound* was exquisitely built in South American cedar (or *cedro*) – said to be harder than its North American equivalent – on South American oak (or *virara*). Just to make sure she survived the south Atlantic storms, each frame was braced to the keel with stainless steel floors and diagonal stainless steel straps were fitted, all of which survive intact to this day.

But perhaps her most unusual feature was the deck. For a start, each plank was locked into its neighbour by means of an angled lap joint, eliminating the need for almost any

RIGHT: Inward Bound's design is identical to the Pilot 35 designed by Sparkman & Stephens, though the company has no record of her being built.

fastenings. More importantly, though, the 1-inch-thick, full-length planks themselves had a rather unusual provenance. About 25 years before she was sunk, the *Belgrano* had been refurbished at a yard in Buenos Aires, where various works were undertaken, including replacing her teak decks with steel ones. The salvaged timber from her redecking no doubt lives on in countless pieces of furniture and window frames around the city, but surely the most appropriate use was on *Inward Bound*, where the deck of one ship was transformed into the deck of another – albeit one almost 1/20th its size!

I caught up with the yacht at the Sparkman & Stephens 75th anniversary celebrations in Mystic Seaport, where she was accorded a place along with 70 other S&S yachts. On board were owner Gary Magwood and first mate Erin Reitav, who had just motor-sailed the yacht down from Lake Ontario via the Erie Canal and the Hudson River. It had taken them 12 days.

A long-time classic boat enthusiast steamboat enthusiast, Gary chartered out an Edwardian launch on the Thames for several years in the 1980s. He also worked with the Caravan Theatre Company when they toured their replica steel Thames barge in Europe, but before acquiring *Inward Bound* had no previous experience of ocean sailing. First mate Erin had learned to sail on board *Inward Bound* and, under the watchful eye of tutor Gary, had been inducted into the fine art of varnishing. She was largely responsible for keeping the yacht's varnish up to scratch – no mean task considering the seeming acres of brightwork glowing in the evening sun.

After a lobster dinner to celebrate 75 years of S&S designs, I joined *Inward Bound* the following day for the next part of the celebrations: an 18-mile cruise in company down the Mystic River to Fishers Island. On the way, Gary told me more about his charge's unusual history.

As *Baraccuda*, the yacht had for several years enjoyed a successful racing career sailing out of the Yacht Club of Argentina, including several wins in the Buenos Aires to Rio Regatta. It was perhaps inevitable that such a seagoing vessel would eventually venture further afield, however, and it was only a question of whether an owner would head south and through the Straits of Magellan to the Pacific or northwards to the Caribbean and, perhaps, North America. The move finally came in 1986 when her then owner, a doctor, was posted to Canada. He decided to take his boat with him and headed on a two-year perambulation of the Caribbean, which saw *Barracuda* finally arrive in Hamilton on Lake Ontario in 1988.

Lake Ontario may not seem an obvious place to take an ocean-going cruising yacht, but at 193 miles long, 53 miles wide at its widest and with 712 miles of coastline, it offers a challenging and varied cruising ground. And, if you want a change of scenery, you can always head east to the famous 1000 Islands Region on the St Lawrence River, which boasts not just 1,000 but 1,800 islands (though I suspect that may include a few pebbles!). It's also the home of a couple of dozen yacht clubs and some serious racing.

Not that Gary had any intention of staying inland. After buying the boat in 1995, he renamed her *Inward Bound* and, after a brief refurbishment at a nearby yard, the following year headed up the St Lawrence River, bound

SPECIFICATIONS

LOA: 35ft 7in (10.9m)
LWL: 24ft 3in (7.7m)
Beam: 9ft 7in (2.9m)
Draft: 5ft 9in (1.8m)
Displacement: 9 tons
Sail area: 528sq ft (49m²)

RIGHT: These decks were made from the decks of the Belgrano *– in fact, most of the boat was built from timber salvaged from the Argentine warship several years before she sank.*

ABOVE: *Far away from her home on the Great Lakes,* Inward Bound *canters across* Fishers Island Sound, *in Connecticut.*

for the Caribbean. It wasn't all plain sailing, however, as 50 miles south of Mahone Bay in Nova Scotia, they were hit by a gale.

'We were running under bare poles and the helmsman Gordon got mesmerised by the compass and didn't see the big one coming from the side,' Gary said. 'We were upside down for 45 seconds. We lost the dinghy, the ports and hatches were smashed, the dodger and a dorade vent were ripped off, and the stanchions and pushpit were bent right over the cockpit like a pretzel. Gordon was washed over the side and spent a terrifying length of time under the boat – he was in such a state of shock he didn't talk for four days afterwards.

'I thought we were sinking and was about to inflate the liferaft when I remembered the old adage, "always step up into a liferaft". The water hadn't risen above the settee berths, so we set the No3 jib on a 350-foot (110-metre) length of line to act as a drogue and started bailing. We removed one of the plywood leeboards and used it to cover the smashed windows. No sooner had the gale abated than we were hit by another one that lasted 14 hours. When we got to Bermuda, 28 hours overdue, I was told I had four broken ribs.'

Despite this experience, Gary went on to have two very good years sailing in the Caribbean before he had to head back to Canada to top up his bank account. By the time he made it back to Lake Ontario, he had sailed some 10,000 miles in the boat.

ABOVE: Inward Bound *is inward bound for Newport, Rhode Island, at the end of the S&S Regatta and cruise.*

Inward Bound was certainly one of the furthest travelled and, with her acres of well-maintained varnish and original chrome bronze fittings, one of the most admired boats at the S&S gathering in Mystic. But I still couldn't help wondering whether she was a real S&S. Who better to ask than the man himself, Olin Stephens, who at 96 years of age was still doing the rounds, still discussing the finer points of yacht design and even chatting to the occasional journalist. Did he have any doubt that *Inward Bound* was one of his? I asked him. 'Oh yeah, she has an interesting history,' he replied. 'I don't remember sending any Pilot drawings to Argentina at that time, but she sure looks like one. She may have been copied, but if she was, she's a very good copy!'

And if it was good enough for Olin, it was good enough for me.

What happened next...

After spending the summer on the East Coast, Gary sailed *Inward Bound* back up to the Great Lakes where he has cruised the Bay of Quinte, The Thousand Islands and Lake Ontario. She remains in almost entirely original condition.

BLUE SALUKI (1964)

THE MODERN ERA

1964 was a transitional time for sailing. In the year that Bob Dylan sang 'The Times They Are a-Changin' ', the French boatyard Bénéteau produced their first fibreglass boat, launching what would become the biggest boatbuilding company in the world. The following year, the American Dick Carter changed the face of yacht design when his revolutionary yacht *Rabbit* – one of the first to have a rudder hanging separate from the keel – trounced all the opposition and won the Fastnet Race.

Lt Cmdr Denis Matthews was having none of it. 'He was a structural engineer, you see,' said his widow Joanna Matthews, speaking 40 years later. 'It was the very early days of fibreglass, and he was dubious about what was then a fairly modern concept. He could foresee structural problems. He wanted a boat for the rest of his life, and was very keen that it should be built of wood.'

Not only was the new yacht to be built of wood, but it was to have a traditional long keel – none of that new-fangled fin keel nonsense for Lt Cmdr Matthews. After an extensive search, the boat he chose was the Prior 37, designed by Alan Buchanan and built by RJ Prior & Son in Burnham. The pretty 37-foot (11.3-metre) Bermudan sloop was launched in August 1964, at a total cost of £6,156 19s 4d, and soon after was certified by Lloyd's as 100 A1. She was outclassed and outdated almost as soon as she touched the water.

Undeterred, Denis Matthews signed up for the first ever Round Britain Race in 1966, with his friend Sub Lt Leslie Williams (EI) RNVR as skipper and had a new Hasler windvane fitted specially for the occasion (costing £200). During the 27-day voyage, the pair suffered exhaustion and a near-knockdown, which Williams later described in typically understated tones:

'We made increasingly good progress until, at 1810, a particularly severe gale broached us to and the spinnaker blew out as we lay with the mast almost horizontal, leaping about on a large swell. We had a real struggle to get the remains aboard as they seemed to wish to act as a drogue astern streamed from the masthead. A highly unsafe

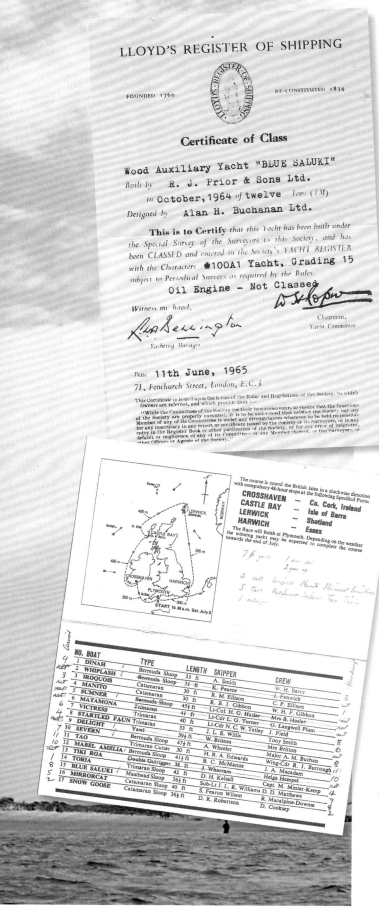

MAIN PICTURE: Blue Saluki's restoration took 2½ years and cost 20 times as much as she cost new.

TOP: She was built to Lloyd's 100 A1 standards.

BOTTOM: The entry list for the Round Britain Race.

situation with a guyed out mainsail still trying to drive us through the water.'

But what the race became famous for was as the first major test of the new, emerging breed of multihull racers – nine of the 17 starters were either trimarans or catamarans. And, despite Williams's protestations about the weather being in their favour, the race results were an overwhelming vindication for the newcomers, with multihulls taking the first six places. *Blue Saluki*, the second monohull over the line, finished a respectable 8th place (7th on handicap). Despite his strong opinions, Lt Cmdr Matthews seems to have been more open-minded than his colleague. 'Denis was very critical of the multihulls,' said Mrs Matthews. 'He was very aware of the stresses and strains and didn't think they'd done enough research. By the end, he was rather impressed and had to acknowledge they were better than he had thought.'

Lt Cmdr Matthews raced his new yacht extensively from 1965 through to most of the 1970s, taking part in at least three Fastnet races and even winning the Dinard Race on one occasion. Mrs Matthews was persuaded to go on board for one Fastnet, though it was not to be repeated. 'I get terribly seasick, so it was a misery to me,' she recalled. 'I kept thinking, we've sailed all this way to Ireland, why don't we stop and enjoy it for a little while!'

But, while her outmoded design may have consigned their beloved yacht to the rear of the fleet on most occasions, the Matthews family cruised *Blue Saluki* extensively for the better part of 20 years. From their base at the Camper & Nicholsons yard in Gosport, they sailed down the West Country, the Channel Islands and visited Brittany on numerous occasions. 'Denis had two daughters from his previous marriage and we had two sons together, who came on board from when they were in carrycots,' remembered Mrs Matthews. 'All they knew about holidays was *Blue Saluki*!'

One of Lt Cmdr Matthews's regular sailing companions was Peter Bathurst, an East Coast sailor who influenced his choice of yard when he was ordering the yacht and who held a small stake in her. After Denis's death in September 1986, Bathurst – keen to keep *Blue Saluki* but unable to maintain her on his own – split the boat's shares into six and formed a syndicate to run her. The Matthews's sons, Alexander and William, became sleeping partners, and three new owners were brought in, although Bathurst always kept the biggest stake. By then, however, Bathurst was in his 80s and, although the boat still occasionally ventured as far afield as the Channel Islands (where one of the partners' brothers lived) and Cherbourg (where cheap booze was aplenty), she was no longer maintained to Denis Matthews's fastidious standards and gradually slipped into disrepair. Significantly, the yacht's last Lloyd's 100 A1 survey was signed off in September 1985, a few months before Denis's death. The situation was aggravated when two of the new syndicate members fell out and refused to sail together.

By the time Bathurst died and the boat was put on the market during the winter of 2001–2002, the yacht that had raced around Britain and survived a near-knockdown was but a memory. 'The deck was shot, the

RIGHT: Charles and Alyson remortgaged their house several times to fund the yacht's restoration.

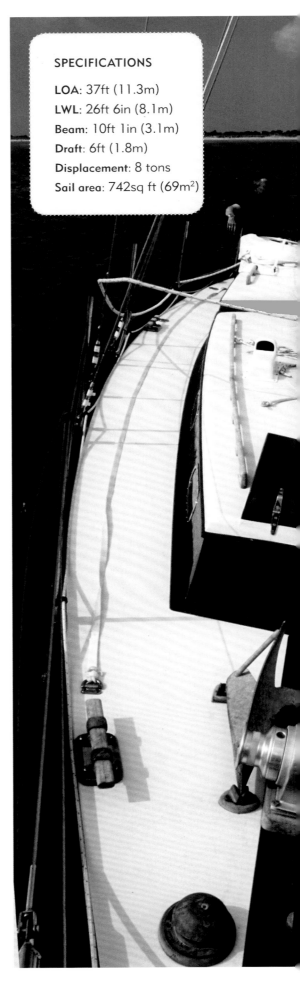

SPECIFICATIONS

LOA: 37ft (11.3m)
LWL: 26ft 6in (8.1m)
Beam: 10ft 1in (3.1m)
Draft: 6ft (1.8m)
Displacement: 8 tons
Sail area: 742sq ft (69m²)

floors were corroded and you could put your finger through the transom. She was hanging on by a wing and a prayer,' said future owner Charles Hurst. 'She was on the market for £25,000 but after one potential buyer dropped out mid survey, they dropped the asking price to £10,000. We eventually got her for £8,000.'

A joiner by trade, Charles had owned and restored several classic boats, working his way up from a 17-foot (5.1-metre) plywood Silhouette to a 25-foot (7.6-metre) Folkboat (the VW Beetle of the sec). But *Blue Saluki* was something else. '*Vashti*, the Buchanan design which the Prior 37 was based on, was my dream boat,' he says. 'But it was *Blue Saluki*'s name that won it for me – it evokes an era when all boats were blue something or another!'

And 'to the era' was very much the ethos that Charles and his partner Alyson embraced during the subsequent restoration at Dolphin Quay in Emsworth, on the south coast of England. For, while they had the yacht's original drawings to work from, there were certain areas they wanted to improve on. For a start, the corroded steel floors and knees were sensibly replaced with bronze, requiring an astonishing 47 castings – 39 floors, two breast hooks and six hanging knees – all beautifully executed by Wessex Castings. Likewise, while the interior layout may have been suited to the mindset of a sixties racer-cruiser, it didn't sit well with the expectations of a noughties cruising couple. The anchor and chain were inconveniently stored under the settee in the saloon, while up in the foc's'le a pair of cot berths folded away to make space for the large and cumbersome 1960s sail wardrobe. By contrast, Charles and Alyson were planning to fit a roller reefing genoa, which meant the only sails they needed stowage for were an asymmetric spinnaker and a storm trisail, freeing up space in the foc's'le for fixed berths and a proper chain locker. At the same time, the chart table was switched from side- to forward-facing.

On the other hand, the couple went to great trouble to refurbish the original fittings wherever possible, such as the stainless steel stanchions and sail track and the tufnol blocks. Where this wasn't possible, they kept very much to the original spirit of the yacht, such as the reading lights sourced from Davey's, made to a traditional design but in plastic. 'I had a firm idea what a boat from this era should look like,' says Charles. 'Because I learned to sail on boats such as the early Van de Stadt designs, and they left a lasting impression.'

But, while the work became almost a personal project for boatbuilder Richard Uttley at Dolphin Quay, it was by no means a chequebook restoration. 'We were originally going to have all the major survey work done by the yard and do the interior ourselves,' says Charles. 'But we worked out that it would be more efficient if I stayed in London and earned the money to pay the yard to do the interior. It was gruelling, coming up with the money, though. I'm only a furniture-maker, and there's only so many kitchens you can make in a week! For the last year, I was working 12 days in London, followed by two days on the boat.'

'We remortgaged our house several time,' adds Alyson. 'Whenever there was a crisis, we would go to the bank and say we needed a new bathroom!'

In the midst of it all, the couple decided to tie the knot. 'We only got married because we wanted the wedding list at the chandler's!' says

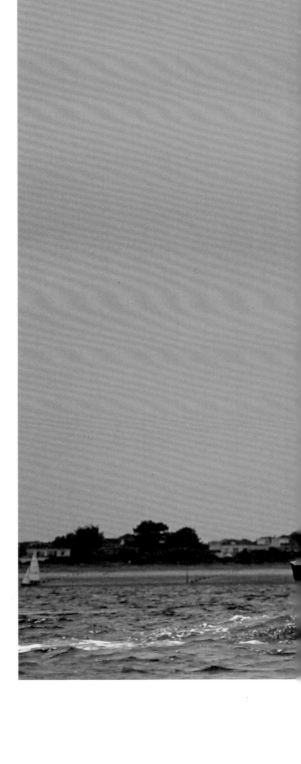

Charles. 'We were absolutely brassic by then, and we got given all the things we couldn't afford at that stage – compass, barometer, berth cushions, echo sounder, log, dan buoy, cutlery, pilot books, charts and even two tins of antifouling. It was fantastic!' The best present of all, however, was the half-model of the yacht built by Richard Uttley using the cedar planking from an old bulkhead that was removed from the boat – an echo, they later discovered, of the scale model Mrs Matthews had given her husband on his 65th birthday some 30 years before.

Two and a half years after Charles and Alyson started work – and after they had spent about 20 times what Lt Cmdr Matthews originally paid for her new – *Blue Saluki* was relaunched in April 2005. In her smart blue and white livery and shiny new rig, she looked every bit a new boat. Yet, look closely and you could see the telltale stains in the varnish and the bronze tops on the stanchions, which were the only clues that most of it is original – just polished up and rebedded. Sure, there were a couple of new cockpit hatches to improve access to the rudder shaft grease gland, and that anchor winch was decidedly not a period fitting, but then she was a boat from the 1960s and not the 1930s, and the distinctions between old and new were therefore that much easier to blur.

For Charles and Alyson, there was no doubt the three years working on the boat had been a formative experience. 'It was a magical time going down at weekends, having cups of tea in the yard. I used to look forward to it all week,' said Charles. 'Because the boat was there so long, people got to know her and would come to see how she was getting on. We learnt so much and made so many friends. It was a fantastic experience – the best thing we've ever done – apart from getting married, of course!'

What happened next...

Charles and Alyson have cruised *Blue Saluki* extensively on the south coast of England and over to Brittany. They've entered the Round the Island Race twice, finishing in mid fleet both times – the same as Lt Cmdr Matthews in 1966.

A TASMANIAN ANGEL

Wooden boats stayed out of fashion throughout most of the Western world for at least 20 years. The revival, when it eventually came, started in the United States in the mid 1970s, travelled to Europe in the mid 1980s and eventually reached Australasia in the mid 1990s. In 1994, the first Australian Wooden Boat Show was held in Hobart, and seven years later I was invited to report on the event for *Classic Boat* magazine. It was one of the highlights of my career as a writer/photographer.

Tasmania is an extraordinary mixture of wildness and civility. The landscape feels huge and careless and free, but the towns are almost Victorian in their primness. It's as if a typical English town had been built in the prairie, or as if this

ABOVE: Heading down the River Derwent after the Australian Wooden Boat Festival, where Madoc was star of the show.

LEFT: Madoc charges across the D'Entrecasteaux Channel, the grass behind parched and yellow in late summer.

great sprawling land was still being tamed by European pioneers. For, make no mistake about it, Tasmania is isolated. The next stop is Antarctica, and walking around Hobart you can't help but be aware you are treading in the footsteps of the great Antarctic explorers who stopped off here on their way to the great ice fields.

Pride of place at the wooden boat festival in 2001 was given to a small but exquisite wooden boat, with a varnished hull and a sign above it saying simply: 'Mike & Wendy, Boatbuilders'. I soon got talking to the aforementioned Mike Seeney and Wendy Edwards, and became fast friends with the intense Englishman and his vivacious Australian wife. A couple of days later, when I mentioned I was keen to visit the south of the island, where large chunks of forest were still left wild, they came up with a tantalising offer.

'The options are to sail with us as far as Kettering, stay the night at our place and borrow our car to drive around the Huon valley,' said Mike. 'You can do any combination, or you can go for the full package. What d'you think?'

There were probably all kinds of things I should have been doing in Hobart to deepen my understanding of Tasmanian maritime history, but

SPECIFICATIONS (ANNIE)

LOD: 24ft (7.3m)
LWL: 21ft 4in (6.5m)
Beam: 8ft 8in (2.6m)
Draft: 3ft 10in (1.2m)
Displacement: 4 tons
Sail area: 333sq ft (31m²)

RIGHT: *Traditional deadeyes and lanyards for the rigging.*

CENTRE TOP: *Mike used only hand tools to build the boat.*

CENTRE BOTTOM: *The tiller curves around the mizzen mast.*

LEFT: *The rigging is tensioned with rope lanyards.*

the call of the sea is not to be denied. I opted for the full package, and a few hours later I was on board *Madoc* (Welsh for 'fortunate one'), drifting down the River Derwent and feeling very fortunate indeed. Behind us the smoke from bush fires swirled apocalyptically over Hobart, while ahead the dry grass of the treeless Lauderdale peninsula beckoned with a startling yellow, casting me back to similar timeless landscapes in Greece. As we had lunch on the scrubbed celery top deck, Mike and Wendy told me about *Madoc* and the unlikely manner of her creation.

It was while on an expedition to the Antarctic on board the converted North Sea trawler *Southern Quest* that, in the age-old tradition of many Antarctic explorers, Mike stopped off in Australia in 1984. And it was in the age-old tradition of lucky escapes that Mike skipped ship in Tasmania, just a few weeks before the *Southern Quest* headed south and sank. The 21 crew on board were all rescued by helicopter, but only after a frightening ordeal on the ice.

Mike's original idea had been to travel back to Europe on his motorbike, but all that changed when his bike was stolen. At this point, most people

*LEFT: Mike and Wendy
sailed the boat as far as Bali
before heading back to 'Tassie'
for good.*

would have just bought another bike or, even simpler, booked a flight home. Instead, Mike decided that, despite having only limited woodworking and sailing experience, it would be a grand idea to build a boat and sail back to England.

He soon spotted a 24-foot (7.3-metre) double-ender called *Annie* (see panel, page 133) he liked the look of and headed down from Sydney, where he had by then found work, to Tasmania, where his tools were stored, to order the timber. A few months later, he was back at Oyster Cove, 40 miles (60km) south of Hobart, faced with 'a pile of tools and timber', which he planned to turn into a boat. It was already a daunting task, but then Mike raised the stakes even further.

As he was attacking the keel with a chainsaw to make the ballast rebate, he suddenly realised how much he hated the noise the machine was making. In a moment of clarity, he put the chainsaw down and decided never to use it again. From then on, he would use only hand tools. 'I wanted to enjoy the process of building the boat,' he said. 'And I realised I would get more enjoyment by learning to use hand tools properly.'

He stuck with his decision, even sawing the planks down their entire lengths to achieve the desired thickness for the hull planking, and using a drawknife to shape the spars for the rig. Back-breaking work surely? 'It wasn't that bad,' said Mike. 'Before I knocked off each day, I would cut a 6 by 2in (152 x 52mm) plank down its length for the planking, so I'd start off fresh the next day.'

Mike used indigenous Tasmanian timbers throughout, although not the Huon pine, which most people assume she is built of – there are only a couple of lengths of the island's most famous wood on *Madoc*. Mostly it's the ubiquitous celery top (a dubious-sounding timber which is in fact a durable boatbuilding material), with spotted gum (a member of the Eucalyptus family) for the ribs.

As well as changing the planking from the carvel (ie edge to edge) specified in the original design to clinker (ie overlapping), Mike made the boat about 4in (102mm) wider – or at least that's how she turned out once the moulds were taken out and the hull sagged ever so slightly. She's also ½in (12mm) wider on one side than the other, which adds a little character...

After four years building the hull and earning his keep by helping to build a boat for the owner of the shed, *Madoc* had her first launching, as a bare hull. From then on, she would be completed in the open on a beach on the other side of the bay. Which is why the planking looks more weather-beaten on the inside of the boat than the outside, having been exposed to the elements for several months before the deck was fitted.

As I watched Mike grinding the beans to make coffee, it occurred to me that the concept of 'enjoying the process' was what informed much of his life, from his decision to build a boat rather than fly home, to having a hot drink. I decided not to tell him that some of my friends insisted on roasting the coffee themselves too – I was already getting impatient for my cuppa.

We were headed south, to the D'Entrecasteaux Channel and the island of Bruny, both named after Bruni D'Entrecasteaux, the French officer who charted the area in 1773. In the 18th century, the channel provided shelter for most of the area's great explorers, such as Abel Tasman (first Westerner to reach Tasmania, in 1642), Cook, Bligh, Flinders and of course D'Entrecasteaux himself. Nowadays, Bruny (in reality two islands joined together by a narrow causeway) is largely a haven for wildlife and tourists, but many of the remnants of the early colonials still survive. The anchorage we were heading for was called Quarantine Bay after the quarantine centre that tested cattle coming into Tasmania from Europe. Two hundred years later, the site was still closed to the public.

Considering his love of 'the process', I was surprised at Mike's eagerness to switch on the engine when we finally reached the D'Entrecasteaux Channel and the wind began to die – in fact, I was surprised there was an engine there at all, all things considered. But things were not always thus.

When *Madoc* was launched for the second time in 1990, she had a flush foredeck, with a hatch amidships and a small cockpit aft. Below decks, there was one big double bunk, with a small seating area and a galley aft. 'When we had dinner parties, people had to sit cross-legged on the bunk,' remembered Mike. She also had no engine.

By then Mike had met Wendy, and the couple cruised around Tasmania without an engine for two years before they decided on some major modifications. *Madoc* was laid up for a year while the interior and the deck layout were redesigned. The cockpit was removed and decked over, and the space below made into a double berth. A proper cabin trunk replaced the hatch, and settee berths were fitted aft of the mast.

At the same time, Mike fitted a trusty single-cylinder 10hp Saab engine, attached to an 18in (457mm) variable pitch propeller ('no need for reverse gear: you just adjust the angle of the blades'). It weighs about a quarter of a ton and has to be hand-cranked (electric start? much too easy!), but Mike was clearly devoted to it. As I watched, he primed it lovingly with oil and demonstrated how it always started first time – it didn't, of course, but I understood what he meant.

The couple lived on the boat for a year in nearby Kettering before finally setting off in 1994 on the journey back to the UK – ten years after Mike had originally arrived in Tasmania. A shortage of funds necessitated a ten-month stopover in Sydney before they headed north to Queensland and Darwin. They were still enjoying the process when they crossed the Timor Sea to Timor and then Bali a year later.

But then something shifted. 'We were faced with crossing the Indian Ocean and realised that once we crossed over, that would be it. We wouldn't be able to come back very easily,' said Mike. 'By then, I was feeling long-distance cruising wasn't really for me. And if we headed back, we could still get our jobs back in Sydney.'

They decided not to sail on and, in an uncharacteristic display of pragmatism, flew back to Sydney. Two friends sailed *Madoc* back to Darwin and from there she was trucked to the east coast. Mike's dream of sailing home to England was over and, perhaps, so was his need to go home. Now married to Wendy, he had Australian citizenship, and the couple began to establish themselves as a mobile boatbuilding service – Wendy having helped Mike with much of the later work on *Madoc* and having built the boat's clinker pram dinghy.

When I met the couple at Hobart, Mike was talking about selling the boat and building something smaller for camper-cruising. But it later emerged that *Madoc* had been on the market several times already – including when she was just a bare hull – and by the end of our sail he once again seemed undecided.

We anchored in Quarantine Bay, about half a cable (300 feet/ 90 metres) away from Bruny Island. We had a cosy meal below decks that evening and, after being rocked asleep by the almost imperceptible motion of the boat, were treated to a spectacular sunrise the following morning. A few hours later, the wind got up from the north just in time for a brisk sail up the channel, before a downpour of surprisingly cold rain rapped on her bare decks.

With its sudden dramatic changes of weather and its wonderfully clear light, Tasmania is a photographer's paradise, and I used up several rolls of film as *Madoc* sailed past me in front of a backdrop of golden grass. She looked absurdly pretty, with her varnished hull, and it was easy to see why she was given pride of place at the Hobart festival. 'We'll have to paint her hull next time,' Mike had joked a few days before, tiring a little of being the centre of attention. Somehow, I couldn't imagine that happening – just as I couldn't imagine him and Wendy ever selling the boat. There are some things that just seem too right to change.

What happened next …

Mike and Wendy sailed on *Madoc* for another ten years, while they built first a straw-bale house and then moved into a 'humpy' on 100 acres of bush. Mike contracted cancer of the colon in 2010, and died the following year. Wendy became a full-time sculptor, while *Madoc* was bought by a local couple who kept her moored on the D'Entrecasteaux Channel.

AMAZING ANNIE

'A very comfortable cruising boat for two people and a small dog' is how the *Annie* design has been described. And, at just 24 feet (7.3 metres) long, the dog really does need to be small. The boat would have seemed even smaller when American designer Fenwick Williams drew it in 1933. Working in the Boston office of John G Alden at the peak of the company's success, Williams was more used to drafting his employer's designs for magnificent 50-foot (15-metre) yachts. With the Depression, however, smaller boats suddenly became more popular, and so 'Fen' drew his chunky little gaff yawl 'on spec'.

The design bears similarities to the working boats of Scotland, while the builder of the original *Annie*, Art Brendze, detected traces of Britain's East Coast bawleys and Falmouth quay punts, and America's Block Island Cowhorn, Eastport Pinky, Isles of Shoals Boat and Hampton Whaler (yes, all these boats do exist!). Suffice to say, the vessel has workboat roots. Brendze found the high-peaked gaff rig 'grossly over-canvassed', and several boats were subsequently rigged as gaff cutters by removing the mizzen mast.

Williams became a successful designer in his own right, based in Marblehead, Mass, and was noted for his catboat designs. His *Annie* plans are still for sale through *Wooden Boat* magazine, 80 years after he originally drew them.

SAVANNAH (1997)

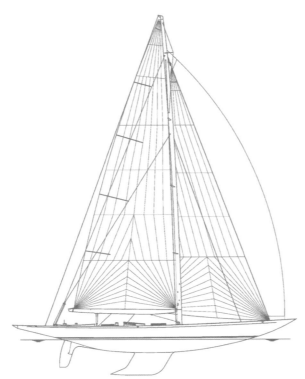

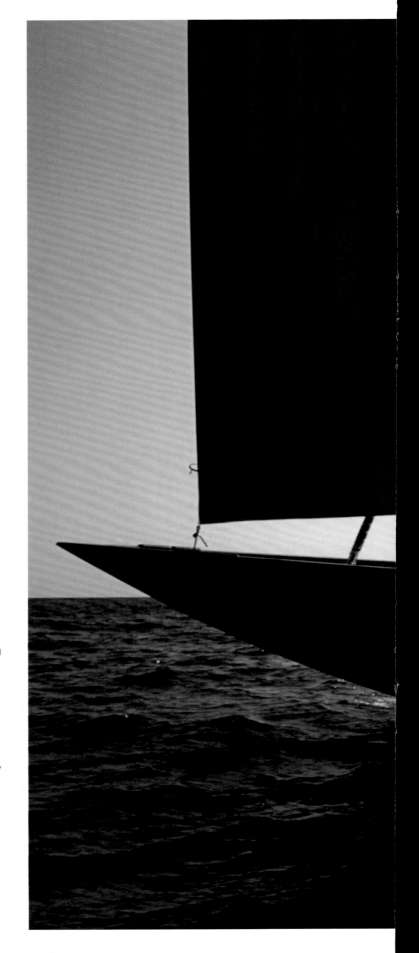

BACK TO THE FUTURE

Time for a recipe. Take the classic aesthetics of yesteryear, add the aerodynamics of a modern hull and a sprinkling of new hardware, mix it all up and bake it in epoxy and carbon fibre, and what do you get? An ersatz boat that doesn't know whether it's old or new, say some. A modern classic, say others. Apart from the controversial use of modern materials such as epoxy and carbon fibre, there's little that has divided the classic boat fraternity more than the advent of the 'modern classic'. It's like showing a red rag to a bull to some aficionados; the merest mention of 'modern' and 'classic' in the same sentence is likely to have them reaching for the caulking mallet to thump you over the head.

The appeal of the type is very apparent, however. If the design is right, you should end up with the 'look' of a classic yacht combined with the performance and ease of handling of a modern boat and without the heavy maintenance schedule of an old boat. What's more, you don't destroy any genuine historic artefacts in the process – something which every purist should be grateful for.

One of the most extreme of this breed of yachts which has challenged the traditionalists at a number of levels was a 90-foot (27-metre) sloop called *Savannah*. The motivation

RIGHT: You need look no further than page 93 to see where the inspiration for Savannah *came from: it's Fife distilled.*

behind her creation was straightforward enough. American millionaire Randolph Watkins simply wanted to build the most beautiful classic-looking yacht he could possibly conceive. He studied the lines of two dozen boats to work out the proportions that make up a perfectly shaped hull, and concluded that the William Fife-designed cutter *Hallowe'en* and the Charles Nicholson-designed J-Class yacht *Endeavour* came nearest to achieving his ideal. Superyacht designer David Pedrick in Rhodes Island was given the brief to realise the concept, and the Concordia boatyard in Massachusetts (builders of the legendary Concordia yawl) was put in charge of building it.

Launched in April 1997, the resulting yacht was little short of breathtaking. With her uncluttered decks and graceful sheer, not to mention 32 feet (9.8 metres) of overhangs, *Savannah* looked like a timeless classic. Soon after her launch, she was awarded the prize for Best Sailing Yacht by Showboats International and the Super Yacht Society.

As *Savannah* lay alongside *Hallowe'en* at the Cannes Régates Royales a few years later, there were clear similarities between the two boats: the long overhangs, the understated sheer, the elegantly rounded stern with its dainty transom. If you didn't know better, the sheer quantity of varnished wood and bare teak decks on *Savannah* might trick you into thinking she was an old classic.

Below decks, *Savannah*'s mahogany panelling gave off a rich glow and the deck beams overhead had a reassuringly solid appearance. But why did those deck beams sound hollow when you knocked them? And why were there no frames lining the inside of the hull? You guessed it. This yacht was built almost entirely of a carbon fibre/foam sandwich, including those deck beams with their beautifully moulded corners. Even parts of the interior joinery were made of wood veneers glued to a foam core as a weight-saving technique.

Underwater, the 70 years of development that divided the two boats were even more apparent. Whereas *Hallowe'en* had the classic long keel of a yacht of her era, with elegant 'wine-glass' sections, *Savannah* had a canoe-shaped hull with a fin keel, in the modern idiom. The older form would provide greater comfort at sea, while the newer boat would undoubtedly be faster and more manoeuvrable.

The numbers said it all. While *Savannah* was undoubtedly bigger than *Hallowe'en*, her proportions were different too. The waterline length, beam and draft were all exactly 18% bigger, but both her displacement and her overall length were 25% bigger. This meant she had even longer overhangs than her illustrious predecessor, more in line with those extreme J-Class yachts she was intended to emulate. The extra weight was simply the result of having a bilge full of watermakers, generators and air conditioning to comply with contemporary standards of luxury. By comparison, *Hallowe'en* was positively spartan.

And then there were the sails. The Bermudan rig had just been discovered when *Hallowe'en* was built, and Fife drew a low-aspect sail plan for his latest design, with a bowsprit and twin foresails to keep the weight of the rig low. Seventy years later, and yacht design has evolved so that *Savannah* could be fitted with a towering carbon fibre mast and narrow sail plan, with no bowsprit and a single foresail set well back from the stem. The result was a

SPECIFICATIONS

LOA: 90ft (27.4m)
LWL: 58ft 4in (17.8m)
Beam: 17ft (5.2m)
Draft: 11ft 6in (3.5m)
Displacement: 43.6 tonnes

LEFT: The controversial Fife dragon carved in Savannah's bow. Sacrilege to some.

ABOVE: Look familiar? Check out pages 102–3 for more Fife inspiration – though Savannah is notably wider.

powerful rig with a long leading edge which allowed the yacht to sail close to the wind – at what her designer described as 'exhilarating speeds'.

It was: 'A tour de force of single-minded aesthetic purity made possible by the intelligent application of modern boatbuilding technology,' said *Boat International USA*.

But all this trickery and doctoring of classic principles was as nothing compared with one small detail that Pedrick and Watkins had incorporated into their design. At the forward end of the cove line, recessed into her hull, they had 'carved' a dragon's head. Now anyone who knows anything about classic boats knows that the dragon's head is the symbol of that great icon William Fife of Fairlie, who after a certain date carved a slightly different dragon into the bows of every boat built at the yard. No one else had ever had the audacity to copy that, and to some it was the final straw. It proved that these boats had no respect for the past.

Randolph disagreed. 'These boats are a tribute to the great boats of the past. They aren't meant to compete against them but only to emulate their example and praise them,' he said. 'The dragon was only meant as a bit of fun and to demonstrate our genuine admiration of Fife.'

I joined *Savannah* for a post-race sail halfway through the Régates Royales, during which the cream of the classic yacht fleet gather for a few days racing off Cannes, in the south of France. The afternoon breeze had begun to fade and the sun had a warm glow as we tacked off the Iles de Lérins. With her canoe-shaped hull, her simple rig and massive wheel you could spin with a single flick of the hand, manoeuvring the 90-foot (27.4-metre) yacht was more like sailing a dinghy – except a lot faster. Even in the lightest of breezes, we were soon doing eight knots, skimming across the deep blue sea with joyful exhuberance.

Perhaps it was because the owner wasn't on board that day and the day's racing was over, or perhaps it was the warmth of the breeze and the scent of lavender drifting off the land. All the debates about what constitutes a classic yacht (that old chestnut!) and the quarrels about a silly dragon carved into the front of a boat felt a long way off. It was just good to be on the water, to feel the bare wood under my feet, and to know that no old boats had been harmed in the making of this thoroughly modern classic. Even old man Fife would probably chuckle at that one.

What happened next...

Savannah was bought by British entrepreneur Hugh Morrison and his partner, fashion designer Amanda Wakeley. The yacht won the Spirit of Tradition class at the Voiles de St Tropez Regatta three years running in 2011, 2012 & 2013. She won her class, division and overall prize at the Spetses Classic Yacht Race in 2014.

The history of a new breed of yacht started in 1976 when designer Bruce King built a 41-foot (12.5-metre) ketch called *Unicorn*. Despite her clipper bow and classic lines, the boat had a thoroughly modern underbody and was built using the latest epoxy technology. Her success led King to design the 92-foot (28-metre) *Whitehawk* with a similar concept, basing her lines on the famous Herreshoff 'masterpiece' *Ticonderoga*. Although there were many that bemoaned this doctoring of the great designer's work, the yacht also drew many admirers and proved fast on the water. Almost by stealth, the era of the modern classic had arrived.

'The line dividing traditional appearance and modern utility is blurred, and therefore requires each of our clients to choose exactly where it is to be drawn,' said King. 'Some of them would love to build a gaff-rigger with bright finished wooden masts, all bronze hardware, etc, but while they dream about it, their pragmatic side generally gains the upper hand, and they wind up with a modern rig, complete with furlers, hydraulic winches, and stainless steel deck hardware. This leaves the geometry of the hull topsides, deck structures, and interior joinery open for traditional treatment.'

A rather different approach was taken by the late Sean McMillan and Mick Newman of Spirit Yachts. For their first boat, they took the attributes of a classic Scandinavian 30-square-metre yacht, gave it a sophisticated lightweight rig and a modern underwater body, and produced a modern speedster with a distinctly retro feel. With her black walnut trim and T-section boom, the

Spirit 37 looked liked nothing else afloat. Yet the concept caught the imagination of a few more discriminating sailors, and gradually the range expanded to include a dozen yachts up to 130 feet (39.6 metres) long.

'When we started, we were just whistling in the dark,' Sean said, remembering the early days of the company when it was refused membership of the British Marine Industry Federation. 'We didn't know if there really was a retro movement. We just built the boat we wanted that was fun and of a size that we could relate to. Luckily, it struck a chord. We're not interested in building pastiches of old yachts. We build out of wood because it's beautiful, but in design terms we are treading a delicate line between moving the boundaries on a bit and staying in the right aesthetic channel.'

ELEONORA (2000)

THE HANDS-ON APPROACH

It could have been obscene – and perhaps to some it was: a rich man's toy created at enormous expense to imitate the grandeur of the past. Decadent, some might say. Yet, despite her enormous size and undoubted cost, there was something strangely understated about the 135-foot (41-metre) schooner *Eleonora*, as she lay at the dock in Falmouth Harbour, Antigua. Whereas most of the yachts around her blinded you with their ostentatious displays of varnished mahogany and shiny deck fittings, she just looked rather neat and tidy and sombre. Almost plain, really. By contrast, the J-Class yacht *Velsheda* looked positively garish, her decks bristling with chrome and stainless steel hardware, like so much expensive cutlery laid out for some high-society dinner. Anyone asked to identify which boat

ABOVE: The mighty fisherman's anchor rests on the yacht's bulwark ready to swing into action.

LEFT: The timeless profile of Herreshoff's schooner Westward *reborn as* Eleonora *70 years later.*

was built in 1933 on visual evidence alone would surely have chosen the brand-new *Eleonora*.

As if to confound my expectations further, I discovered something else unusual about *Eleonora*. Her rigging is made almost entirely of galvanised steel. None of this flashy stainless steel stuff that has become the norm for most classic yacht restorations and new-builds. Just good old-fashioned galvanised steel. This small detail made me look at the boat and, when I later met him, her owner in an entirely different light. It was the first clue to understanding a new-build philosophy which embraces traditional methods not simply for ideological or fashionable reasons but out of good seamanlike common sense. It was also the first hint that *Eleonora*'s owner might not be another rich man 'imitating the grandeur of the past'. Both observations, I was to discover, run to the core of what *Eleonora* is about.

The yacht's builder and first owner, Ed Kastelein, was born of two seafaring families. On his mother's side the family owned the Holland–America Line, while for 300 years his father's family had made their money from commercial fishing. True, his grandfather was more interested in fashion while his father himself started a chain of bakeries but, as we shall see, Ed has more than made up for this temporary aberration. The obsession started young, with Ed building his first boat, a four-plank canoe made from pieces of salvaged timber, at the age of 12. Even then his hobby was yoked to an equally inborn head for business, and it wasn't long before he was buying boats, doing them up and selling them on at a profit. Either that, or building them from scratch, sailing them and then selling them. It was a pattern that would continue, even as the boats themselves got ever bigger and ever more ambitious.

After taking a few years out to set up a successful chain of restaurants and hotels, Ed came back to the sea, first building a 52-foot (16-metre) double-ender which he sailed to the Med, then managing a chain of increasingly ambitious restoration projects, including the 100-foot (30-metre) ketch *Aile Blanche* and the 119-foot (36.5-metre) ketch *Thendara*. Ed was closely involved either as project manager or doing the work himself and, once completed, each boat was made to pay for itself through either charter work or resale.

Then one day he came across Errol Flynn's old boat *Zaca* hauled out of the water in Villefranche on the Côte d'Azur. Ed was captivated by the yacht's rakish shape. He soon realised she was too far gone to restore, however, and decided instead to build a new boat loosely based on her lines and those of the Grand Banks schooners in general. The 121-foot (36.9-metre) schooner *Zaca a te Moana* was the result.

It was a spectacular achievement, the culmination of years of patient ambition, and most sensible folk would have left it at that. But not Ed. After a few years' chartering in the Mediterranean, he was ready for a new challenge. 'After I sold *Zaca*, I thought of doing something completely different, maybe nothing to do with boats, such as rebuilding a castle in the south of France,' Ed said. 'But then I started to read about *Westward*. I thought, this boat is really sensational; she's fast, beautiful and with a big history. I looked at other designs, but I kept coming back to *Westward*. I couldn't get her out of my mind.'

SPECIFICATIONS

LOD: 136ft (41.5m)
LWL: 96ft (29.3m)
Beam: 26ft 10in (8.2m)
Draft: 17ft (5.2m)
Displacement: 209 tons
Sail area: 11,840sq ft
(1,100m²)

RIGHT: Viewed from a helicopter, the yacht's mass of rigging and endless deck details become apparent.

INSET: The pinrails are based on Herreshoff's design, with struts added to give extra strength.

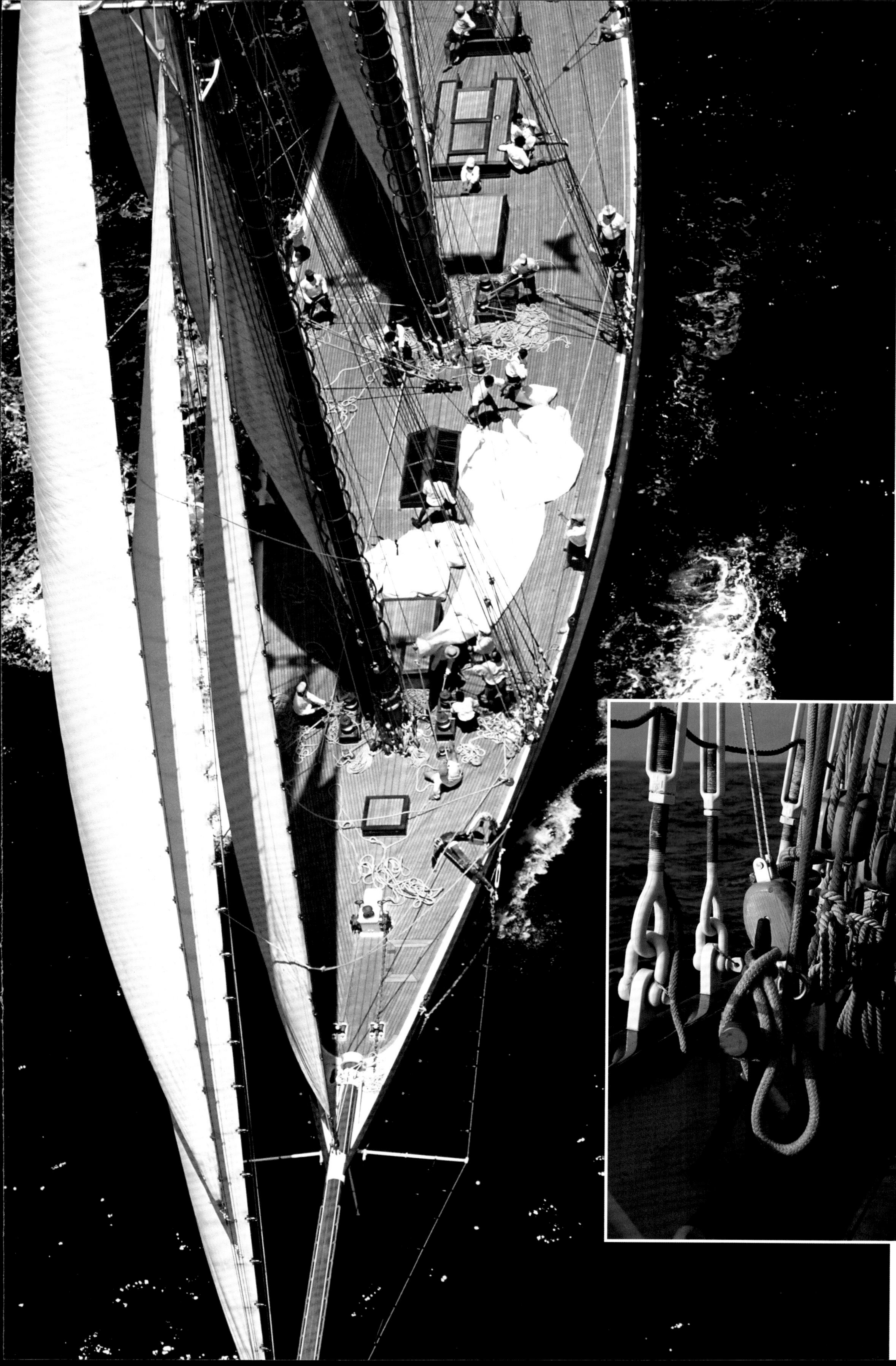

Before long he had decided: he would build a new boat to the same lines Herreshoff's famous 1909 design, winner of 11 out 11 races in her first year and generally acknowledged to be the fastest schooner of her day (see panel, page 149). First, however, he had to find a designer who would adapt the original design to modern requirements without losing the essence of the design. 'Most of the designers I spoke to wanted to put their signature on the boat, to change it somehow, but I didn't want it changed,' said Ed. 'Eventually I found a firm in Holland which is technically proficient but know that in terms of aesthetics they cannot do better than Herreshoff.'

But while the overriding principle might have been 'we cannot do better than Herreshoff', there were certain practical alterations which the Gaastmeer design firm had to take on board. For a start, *Westward* was originally designed without an engine, so a hole had to be cut in the rudder for the propeller. The hull construction itself was also updated from riveted steel to welded steel plates. Below decks, modern safety regulations required several waterproof bulkheads to be installed, which in turn dictated much of the cabin layout. So, whereas *Westward*'s foc's'le was an open space fitted with rows of cot bunks for her 33 crew, the new boat had three cabins, a mess and a galley for her six crew. And, while *Eleonora* still boasted the exact same number of portholes as the original design (20 each side), modern regulations stated they had to be sealed shut, rather than the traditional opening type. Modern standards of comfort also meant that Herreshoff's original 6-foot (1.8-metre) bunks had to be stretched to something a little more accommodating. In the end, an entirely new interior was created, although many original details were copied from the *Westward*. Amazingly, all the wood for the interior – apart from the table in the crew's mess – came from a single 57ft by 8ft 3in (17.4 x 2.5m) log of African mahogany, plus the odd sheet of plywood.

Significant alterations were also made to the rig. While *Westward* needed the combined strength of 31 crew to handle her 13,500sq ft (1,250m²) of racing canvas, nowadays the practicalities of chartering with a relatively small crew dictate a slightly more modest cloud of sail. *Westward*'s 'cruising' rig provided a more manageable alternative, with the main boom at around 71ft (21.6m) instead of 84ft (25m) – although the new boat still carried a pretty majestic 11,840sq ft (1,100m²) of sail.

This pragmatic approach to the original design was evident on deck in countless small details, from the pinrails to the cranse iron, where original Herreshoff fittings provided the starting point and, where necessary, were subtly adapted. Some alterations were larger than others, such as the cabin trunk just forward of the helm, which was fitted with a curved bench and, frankly, looked much more graceful than *Westward*'s plain old box. In fact, most of the trunks had to be repositioned to fit in with the new cabin layout. The majority of fittings on board were custom-made, however, to ensure they were as faithful to Herreshoff's designs as possible – there was very little that was 'off the shelf' on this yacht.

All these alterations meant the boat ended up some 15 tons lighter than the original – a weight saving soon absorbed by all the extra 'mod cons', such as a 460hp Baudouin engine with 1,650 gallons (7,500 litres) of fuel,

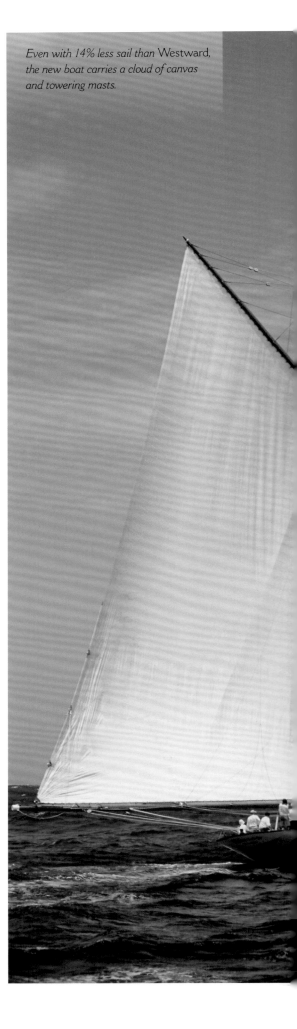

Even with 14% less sail than Westward, *the new boat carries a cloud of canvas and towering masts.*

two generators, air conditioning, a watermaker, not to mention a radar, Inmarsat telecommunications system, Navtex, personal computer, etc, etc.

And then there was that galvanised rigging. Ed insisted they use galvanised for solid practical reasons. 'It wasn't only a question of aesthetics,' he said. 'Galvanised rigging is much more reliable. You can see straight away if it starts to deteriorate, whereas stainless steel after 20 years still looks perfect but might be about to break, so you have to replace the whole lot just in case.' Like so many other details aboard *Eleonora*, practical common sense walked hand in hand with sound aesthetic judgement to produce a solution that was just right for the boat.

But was *Eleonora* a replica of *Westward*? It was an issue close to Ed's heart, as became apparent as soon as I mentioned the 'R' word. 'Replica is not the right word,' he quickly corrected me. 'If I buy a Rolex, it's not a replica of the original Rolex; it's just a Rolex. A hundred years ago, if they built a boat to the same design as another, it wasn't called a replica, it was just a new boat. *Eleonora* was built to the same lines as *Westward*, but she's a different boat. That's why we gave her a different name. We made that mistake with *Zaca a te Moana*. By giving her that name, everyone assumed she was a replica of Errol Flynn's boat and were disappointed when they discovered she was a new boat. *Eleonora* is just *Eleonora*, a schooner built to a Herreshoff design and inspired by *Westward* and her near-sister ship *Elena*.'

The hottest tickets in town at the 2003 Antigua Classic Yacht Regatta was the champagne and rum punch party on board *Eleonora*, where the owner himself was on hand to pour out the bubbly. Ed was polite and businesslike as we made arrangements for me to join the ship on the passage to St Martin, 150 miles north of Antigua, before she crossed the Atlantic to France for the start of the Mediterranean season. Then, as we shook hands to say goodbye, something else struck me about this man. Unlike most superyacht owners, whose closest contact with timber is usually the boardroom table, Ed's hand had the roughness which is generally earned only through regular and intimate contact with the boat's structure.

It was another small detail, but one that summed up the difference between *Eleonora* and most other yachts of her ilk. She was a boat run as a business that earned her keep through charter work before eventually being sold on to make way for the next Kastelein enterprise (see page 148). And Ed was every bit the hands-on owner, overseeing every aspect of her construction as her project manager, and even helping out with some of the manual tasks. Once the boat was launched, he took on the role of skipper and the boat didn't go anywhere without him on board.

This egalitarian approach reminds me of the old *Westward*'s original owner, Alexander Cochran. After the yacht's first, triumphant season in Europe, he is said to have sat down one day and worked out how much the boat had cost him up until that point. He then divided the total by the number of employees at his carpet factory and wrote each of them a cheque to demonstrate his gratitude for what they, through their loyal service, had made possible.

Or *Westward*'s final owner, TB Davis. Whereas most yacht owners of the era employed a crew only for the duration of the sailing season, after which they were dismissed and the vessel handed over to a boatyard for

maintenance, 'TB' kept his crew on all year round and had them do all the maintenance, including making new sails. He is also said to have shinned halfway up the yacht's mast without a bosun's chair, and was once told by King George V, whose *Britannia* he raced against regularly, that: 'I always say you are the only sailor in the fleet.' Praise indeed.

My passage to St Martin aboard *Eleonora* was not quite what I had hoped for, as a dearth of wind meant we ended up motoring all the way. The only salt to touch those glorious wide decks was from the buckets of sea water used to flush away the entrails of a king fish caught and disembowelled by Nilo the deckhand. But the trip did confirm an impression I gained while observing the yacht from the (dis)comfort of the press boat: that of a tight-knit crew working together with silent efficiency. There was no shouting, barely a raised voice in fact, and yet everyone knew exactly what to do.

Ed was more voluble, however, when it came to discussing the ethics of the classic racing circuit – and, more specifically, the general attitude to 'modern classics' such as *Eleonora*. 'It's ridiculous to put a boat like *Eleonora* in the Spirit of Tradition class,' he said. 'Of course she's a new boat, but she's almost exactly the same as the boat launched 100 years ago. She has just as much right to be in the classic class as an old boat that has been rebuilt just keeping one little bit of rust so that people can say it's the original. That's not what's important. What's important is that people should be encouraged to bring more boats like this back on the water.'

Indeed, though the paint on his new yacht had barely dried, Ed was already thinking about his next project. And there was only one boat that could possibly compete with *Westward*: the mighty schooner *Atlantic*, also skippered by the legendary Charlie Barr and whose 1905 transatlantic record stood unbeaten for 97 years.

Meanwhile, sitting on deck of *Eleonora*, the glow of the evening sun setting the varnish aglow as the island of St Kitts vanished away on one side and St Martin appeared on the other, Ed was full of enthusiasm for his latest creation. And, despite all the changes he had made, he was confident that the Wizard of Bristol (aka Herreshoff) would approve of the yacht too. As he puts it: 'I'm sure if Herreshoff came on board *Eleonora* he would see all the details and would say, "This is my boat."'

What happened next...

The 185ft (56m) schooner *Atlantic*, built by Ed Kastelein, was launched in 2008 and completed her sail trials in June 2010. The following year, she won Best Yacht in the 45m+ category at the Superyacht Awards.

TOP LEFT: A functional deckhouse turned into an elegant seat.

CENTRE LEFT: Most of the rigging is galvanised steel.

BOTTOM LEFT: Compass and binnacle based on the original.

RIGHT: Even the bollard cleats are period copies.

THE INSPIRATION

It took three charges of explosives to sink the mighty schooner *Westward*. The owner's last wish was clear: if no suitable buyer was found after his death, the yacht should be destroyed rather than end her life in ignominy. So, on 15 July 1947, *Westward* was taken to the Hurd Deep just north of the Casquets in Jersey and, without further ado, ritually sunk. It was the end of 37 years of racing during which the boat had established herself as one of the greatest names in yachting history.

Nat Herreshoff's design No 692 was launched on 31 March 1910. Designed to the Universal Rule for wealthy New York businessman Alexander S Cochran, the 328-ton yacht was at the time the largest vessel built by the Herreshoff yard. Despite being intended for racing, she is said to have been fitted with a grand piano. A month after being launched, she sailed to Europe with the legendary Charlie Barr at the helm to take on the rest of the Big Class.

Accounts of her performance vary and there seems to have been some controversy over her rating, with Cochran wanting to race to the rule to which she was built and the Europeans insisting on their rating system. Whichever way you look at it, however, she was spectacularly successful, winning 11 out of 11 races on the water and conceding only one on handicap. Triumph in Europe was followed by similar success back in the United States, where she won the coveted Astor Cup the following season.

Westward's first winning streak came to an end with the death of her first skipper in 1911. With Charlie Barr gone, Cochran's enthusiasm for sailing waned, and he put the yacht on the market the following year. She was quickly snapped up by a German syndicate and, renamed *Hamburg II*, resumed her sparring with the Kaiser's yacht. After the war, *Westward* was seized by Britain as a war prize and sold to Clarence Hatty, who restored her to her original name.

The second great period of the yacht's life started in 1924, when she was bought by Thomas Benjamin ('TB') Davis, a South African sportsman/sailor based in Jersey. Under her sailing master Alf Diaper, *Westward* raced at most of the major regattas in Britain as well as taking part in regattas in Norway and France, each winter returning to her berth in Jersey. One of her regular rivals was the King George's *Britannia*, against whom she is said to have raced 174 times. Eleven years after *Britannia* was scuttled off the Isle of Wight, *Westward* joined her to the same watery grave.

INTEGRITY (2012)

THE NEW VICTORIAN

Anyone asked to name the most outstanding classic yacht restorations of the past 20 years is likely to include two boats on their list: the 1885 Camper & Nicholsons cutter *Marigold* and the 1885 Beavor-Webb cutter *Partridge* (see page 8). Yet, while there has been a steady stream of replicas of pretty West Country gaffers and spectacular J-Class yachts, few people have attempted to copy this particular type of vessel. Perhaps it's because this quintessential Victorian design, with its overhanging stern, narrow beam and excessive draft, is no longer deemed practical for this day and age. With most marinas charging by length, you need a boat that's short and fat, rather than long and narrow, to optimise your berth space.

Will Stirling, however, is an idealist. He spent two years researching the design and construction of 18th–19th-century revenue cutters when he built his first major project, *Alert*. He subsequently sailed the vessel, with its dipping lug mainsail, to Iceland, and was prevented from sailing her further only by the imminent arrival of his firstborn. When it came to designing his next boat, he looked back to the distinctive craft that defined the early years of British yacht design.

'The design of *Integrity* was inspired by well-known boats such as Nicholson's *Marigold*, Beavor-Webb's *Partridge*, Watson's *Vanduara* and Dixon Kemp's *Zoraida*. The straight-stemmed cutters of this era are particularly graceful,' he said. 'But whereas with my first boat I was trying to duplicate an exact historic type, I had a bit more leeway this time. Designers are always trying out different things on yachts. So with the shape of the cockpit, for instance, I could play around and see what worked best, without being tied to a specific historic shape.'

Despite such apparent leeway, Will has been meticulous in his research and you get the feeling that every component of the boat had been thoroughly investigated before he even lifted pencil to paper. Take the rig, for instance. That topsail yard might look the same as *Partridge*'s topsail yard to you and me, but Will was quick to point out that the angle of the yard to the topmast changed in about 1880–1885, so that

RIGHT: Not a restoration nor a replica but a new design inspired by some of the 'greats' such as Partridge *(see page 8).*

the spar on boats built before then (eg *Vanduara*) were more angled than on boats built afterwards (eg *Partridge*). *Integrity*'s rig, he assured me, was the older plan.

Despite this minor qualification, the design he produced looked remarkably like *Partridge*, with her low sheer and rather austere stem. Yet the figures told another story. *Partridge* was just 10ft 6in (3.2m) wide for her 49ft (14.9m) length on deck (LOD) – practically 'plank on edge' – whereas *Integrity* was 11ft (3.4m) wide for her 43ft (13.1m) LOD. Despite being an altogether smaller boat, then, *Integrity* was actually beamier than *Partridge*. There were other significant differences too: Will's boat had a more sweeping sheer, higher topsides, a more rounded forefoot and a wider stern. The result was a pleasing compromise, which looked every bit like a Victorian gentleman's yacht but was less likely to heel over at the slightest breeze and to act like a submarine in a big sea – the true 'plank on edge' designs were notoriously tender and wet.

'It's great looking back, because you can pick and choose,' said Will. 'You can look back at different aspects of design and make a judgement about what worked and what didn't, and improve the bits that didn't.'

But while Will might have moderated the design somewhat, he was uncompromising in his choice of building materials. *Integrity* was traditionally built from larch planking on sawn oak frames, spaced 15 inches (380 millimetres) apart, with alternate bronze and oak floors, all fastened with copper and bronze. The decks were of solid Columbian pine – indeed, Will seemed slightly outraged when asked if there was a plywood subdeck – and the deck furniture was opepe with oak trim.

SPECIFICATIONS

LOD: 43ft (13.1m)
LWL: 37ft (11.3m)
Beam: 11ft (3.4m)
Draft: 7ft 6in (2.3m)
Displacement: 21 tons
Sail area: 2,000sq ft (186m²)

ABOVE LEFT: The frames were hewn from oak crooks using a chainsaw. Not a job for the faint-hearted.

ABOVE RIGHT: Casting the lead keel, wearing a mask to protect against the fumes.

OPPOSITE PAGE
TOP: Will stained the interior wood using Van Dyke crystals made from walnut husks, before sealing it with beeswax.

BOTTOM: Will's first sight of the actual boat: frames fitted, a couple of planks to show the line, and the deck dummied up. Perfect.

Likewise, the hull was caulked with cotton and putty, and the deck sealed with traditional pitch. And he assured me there was absolutely no plywood in her whatsoever.

Will was also faithful to many other period details. Her deck planks, for instance, were all individually tapered to follow the curve of the hull, and most run in a single line all the way from the stern to the bow, with only a few planks being 'nibbed' into the side plank (ie 'covering board') forward of the mast. It's a feature Will spotted on *Partridge* and decided to replicate on his boat, despite the extra work involved. 'It's a Victorian aesthetic which has little regard for labour,' he says. 'Working out the maths is a complete nightmare!'

He also designed and had made patterns for most of the bronze deck fittings, including the cleats, deck eyes and fairleads (the latter identical to those on *Partridge*). He even made the mainsheet buffer from scratch, casting the nuts and bolts and oversize shackles, and spacing them with giant rubber washers. The anchor winch, too, was assembled using elements of an old winch combined with parts Will had specially cast or welded himself to produce exactly the machine he wanted with a two-gear mechanism: a 'high' gear for breaking out the anchor, and a 'low' gear for winching in the chain.

Will took a similar approach below decks. In keeping with the period, the accommodation was lavishly fitted out with oak panelling and the requisite buttoned leather settees in the saloon. It was all beautifully crafted with lots of attention to detail, such as the curved ladder steps with a space on the inside to allow the water through, and the delicately curved leaf supports under the saloon table which marry in perfectly with the curve on the sides of the legs.

One cheeky detail some eagle-eyed classic yacht aficionados would later pick up on was the date carved into the yacht's stern. Below her name, where yachts such as *Partridge* have the year of their launching, Will carved the figure '1879', even though the yacht was launched in 2012. There were some who suggested he was trying to pass off his Victorian-inspired design as a genuinely old boat, but he brushed this notion aside, saying: 'I did it to prevent confusion. Someone who doesn't know about the history of yacht design might look at the boat and not understand why it looks the way it does. The date is meant to indicate the era the design is based on – it wasn't meant to hoodwink people into thinking she was built then.'

It took Will and his team just over two years to build *Integrity*, after which the boat had to be trailed for 30 miles to a suitable launching place in Plymouth – a feat which necessitated lopping a few branches along the way with a chainsaw. Launched on 12 June 2012, she was officially named by Will's mother, Elizabeth Barlow, two weeks later. The ceremony took place just a few hundred yards away from where, 214 years before, Elizabeth's own great-great-great-grandmother, Eliza Barlow, had named the HMS *Foudroyant*. The 80-gun warship went on to have an illustrious career, including serving for two years as Nelson's flagship.

A week after *Integrity* was christened, Will sailed her up to Cowes for the annual British Classic Yacht Club Regatta. Although he had no intention of racing, Wednesday was Challenge Day, and *Integrity* was duly challenged by two other comparable yachts: *Thalia*, a 45-foot (13.7-metre) Victorian cutter, and *Aeolus*, a 42-foot (12.8-metre) 'plank on edge' cutter from California. It was a dramatic day, with thunder and lighting exploding all around and hail gathering on the deck. At one point there was so much rain, the crews couldn't see the next mark. Despite the atrocious conditions and having only a borrowed crew, *Integrity* won convincingly on only her fourth outing ever. A few weeks later, she picked up the Best Boat Trophy and was named People's Choice at the Plymouth Classics. It was a good beginning for the plucky West Country upstart.

There was the calm before the storm when I sailed on board *Integrity* off Plymouth one August weekend. A great bank of clouds was piled up in the west, but the sea was glassy calm and the wind seemed to be holding its breath. *Integrity* managed to find a puff of air, and ghosted past Drake's Island towards Kingsand. Never one to duck a challenge, Will took the opportunity to strip off and somersault off the yacht's stern – now turned diving board – into the chilly water.

It was a typically English scene, until the sky cleared from the east and a sea breeze sprang up from the south. In a matter of minutes, the picture was transformed, as *Integrity* reached out over an expanse of bright, sparkling wavelets. Suddenly, I had a feeling of déjà vu and was transported

RIGHT: The closest thing you'll get to this view is on page 15, though 137 years separate the two boats.

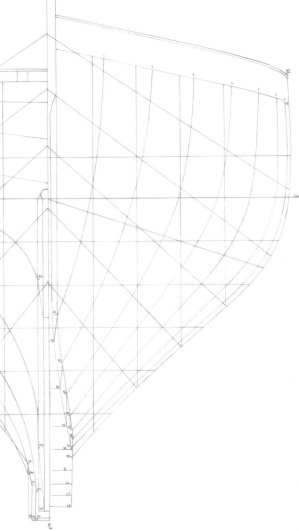

back to Cannes, ten years earlier, photographing *Partridge* as she sliced through the dazzling sea off the Iles de Lérins. The resemblance was uncanny, although *Integrity*'s more rounded shape marked her out as the more modern yacht – and, dare I say it, the prettier, to my eyes.

I took the helm a few days later, on my second outing. Will had carved a mighty tiller, with a cuboctahedron (that's a cube with the corners cut off) apparently inspired by Dixon Kemp, and the impression was of steering a much larger vessel – or was it that her 7-foot 6-in (2.3-metre) draft made her slightly heavy on the helm? Not that she was sluggish – quite the opposite. With her jackyard topsail up, she set nearly 1,500 square feet (140 square metres) of sail, which pushed her along nicely in the gentlest of breezes.

As you'd expect of a Victorian gaff cutter, *Integrity* didn't like sailing too close to the wind, and was at her best off the wind. That said, Will judged that, during the BCYC race on the Solent, his boat pointed slightly higher and was slightly faster to windward than her challenger *Thalia* – evidence that his retrospective tinkering with Victorian design principles might have paid off.

Will achieved a rare thing in *Integrity*. He managed to design a yacht which was imbued with the character of a period yacht without becoming a slave to history. *Integrity*'s sheer was as sweet and clean as any yacht designed during that era, and yet the whole boat had its own distinct 21st-century personality. It was an astonishing achievement for only his second major build, and one which promised well for not only his future but the future of wooden boatbuilding as a whole.

What happened next...

Integrity was voted the Best New Build Over 40 feet in the 2013 Classic Boat Awards. The same year, Will took over the lease of the historic Slip No1 at Devonport, the very place where Eliza Barlow launched Nelson's flagship the *Foudroyant* in 1798. He launched his 15ft (4.6m) expedition boat in 2014 and sailed it around Godrevy lighthouse in Cornwall, as part of a bid to sail around every offshore lighthouse in the UK.

BELOW: Integrity *sails across Plymouth Sound a few weeks after being launched. What could be a prettier sight?*

It was while driving his Mobylette over the Alps to Turkey that Will Stirling designed his first yacht. By day, he drove the 50cc moped from village to village, occasionally pausing to admire the scenery and sample local delicacies, while every evening he pulled out a pile of books from his rucksack and dived into a world of buttocks, diagonals and offsets. He was particularly drawn to the 19th-century revenue cutters and yachts based on them – such as the 1819 cutter *Pearl*, built by former Essex smuggler Philip John Sainty.

By the end of the three-month trip, he had designed his own 37-foot (11.3-metre) smuggling boat, based not on the lines of any one craft but on the amalgamation of the many boats he had studied from that period. The result was *Alert*, a clinker-built, two-masted lugger with a distinctly 'period' look about her, with her upright stem and lute stern.

That Will was attracted to the type is perhaps not surprising, bearing in mind his great-great-great-great-great-grandfather (or 'very great grandfather', as he puts it) was Admiral Sir Robert Barlow, a British naval officer who saw valiant service during the American and French Revolutionary Wars. Barlow has the distinction of being the first officer to capture an armed ship from the French Republic, a privateer called *Le Patriote*, which he seized on 2 January 1793, a month before France officially declared war on Britain.

Sailing, then, and in particular the romantic but little-known world of revenue cutters and smugglers, are in Will's blood. So too is a certain spirit of derring-do – or at least a complete inability to think that anything isn't possible, providing you throw your all at it. You might call it the 'Eton effect' (Eton being the expensive private school where Will studied along with the likes of Princes William, Boris Johnson and Bear Grylls), or the effect of being related, if only by marriage, to Britain's greatest naval commander, Horatio Nelson (Robert Barlow's daughter Hilaire married Nelson's older brother William).

Even when he's not off on some daring expedition to the frozen north, Will is dreaming up other challenges, such as building a 14-foot (4.3-metre) dinghy and sailing across the Channel for the fun of it (or, as he puts it, because 'contrast sharpens one's appreciation of circumstance'). Or sailing the same dinghy around the Eddystone Lighthouse, 12 miles off Plymouth, to raise money for Water Aid (the stunt raised £820). Or building a replica of the *Beagle* to sail through the Magellan Straits (this last one is still just a dream).

INDEX

ACKNOWLEDGEMENTS

Twenty boats over 20 years – that's a lot of helping hands to thank. To start at the beginning: Thanks to Alex Laird for providing inspiration for me and many others through his amazing work on *Partridge*; and to Arthur van't Hoff for not only commissioning an article about *Partridge* back in 2000 (and thereby giving me the courage to go freelance) but also translating it back from Dutch to English for this book when I couldn't find the original file! To Dominic Ziegler for his help with *Marian*'s archive pics (we got there in the end!). Thanks to Federico Nardi at the Cantiere Navale dell'Argentario and Doug Peterson for help with *Bona Fide*'s history, Giuseppe Giordano for inviting me on board, and James Robinson Taylor for the restoration pics (good luck with that book mate!). Thanks to Johan Petersen for the trip of a lifetime on board *Stavanger* and the loan of a fabulous lens, and the crew of *Harald V* for driving me home! Thanks to Richard Oswald for making it real with *Coral of Cowes*, and Charlie Couture for the interior pics. The *Rawene* story wouldn't have been possible without Mark Bartlett and Hamish Ross to get me out to New Zealand, Sandra Gorter to guide me, the Brooke brothers to take me out sailing, and of course Jack Gifford to keep the flame alive for so long. Thanks to skipper Peter Mandin for letting me on board *The Lady Anne* (eventually!), and to Duncan Walker at Fairlie Restorations for supplying plans and photos of the restoration. Thanks to Giuseppe and Elisabetta Longo for their help and hospitality with my *Lulworth* report, and to Cpt Gerald Read and crew for taking me out despite the inclement weather. The *Brilliant* story wouldn't have been possible without the insights of Kristen Kuczenski and the late George Moffett. Thanks to Federico Nardi and Giles McLoughlin for help with the *Stormy Weather* story, and of course the late Olin Stephens for being so generous with his time. Tony McGrail was the perfect host on *Bloodhound*. Thanks to Robert Daral and Jean-Paul Guillet for taking me on *Vanity V*'s re-inaugural cruise, Guy Ribadeau Dumas for historic research, and Marc Pajot for sailing tactics. Iain McAllister provided invaluable research for the *Solway Maid* story, and owner Rodger Sandiford a steady hand at the helm. Thanks to Marina Coutarelli, Stratis Andreadis and the organisers of the Spetses Classic Yacht Regatta for sponsoring my trip to Greece, and to Nikos Riginos for taking me out on the wonderful *Faneromeni*. Skipper Gary Magwood and first mate Erin Reitav provided a warm welcome on board *Inward Bound*. Thanks to Charles and Alyson Hurst for entrusting me with their priceless *Blue Saluki* documents. Wendy Edwards and the late Mike Seeney were unstinting in their generosity when I sailed on *Madoc*. Thanks to Randolph Watkins and his crew for hoisting me up *Savannah*'s mast to take some of my career best photos. Ed Kastelein and his crew gave me a memorable ride to St Martin – shame there wasn't any wind! Thanks to Will and Sarah Stirling for persevering with everything despite the West Country weather…

All pictures by Nic Compton except: p9 (plans), p11 (archive photo), p12–13 (all) courtesy Alex Laird; p16 courtesy Dominic Ziegler; p20–1 (all) Chris Viles; p23 (sail plan) Ed Burnett; p23 (photo) www.timloftusboatbuilding.co.uk; p24 (inset) courtesy Cantiere Navale dell'Argentario; p28–9 (all) James Robinson Taylor; p31 (archive photo) Beken of Cowes; p34–5 (all) courtesy Norwegian Society for Sea Rescue (NSSR); p39 (plans) Norwegian National Maritime Museum; p46 (both) Charlie Couture; p47 (archive photo) classic.sp-yachts.com; p50 (all) & p51 (sail plan) Robert Brooke; p60 (all) courtesy Fairlie Restorations; p68 (sail plan) Stefano Faggioni; p80–1 James Robinson Taylor; p84–91 (top) Gary Blake; p91 (bottom) Marc Millar; p94 (sail plan) Guy Ribadeau Dumas; p99 & p104 (lines & sail plan) courtesy Rodger Sandiford; p108–9 Nikos Riginos; p132–3 (plans) courtesy WoodenBoat (plans available from www.woodenboat.com); p134 (sail plan) Pedrick Yacht Designs; p152–3 (all) & p154 (plans) Will Stirling.